The French Educator
Célestin Freinet (1896-1966)

An Inquiry into How His Ideas Shaped Education

VICTOR ACKER

LEXINGTON BOOKS

A division of
ROWMAN & LITTLEFIELD PUBLISHERS, INC.
Lanham • Boulder • New York • Toronto • Plymouth, UK

LEXINGTON BOOKS

A division of Rowman & Littlefield Publishers, Inc.
A wholly owned subsidiary of The Rowman & Littlefield Publishing Group, Inc.
4501 Forbes Boulevard, Suite 200
Lanham, MD 20706

Estover Road
Plymouth PL6 7PY
United Kingdom

British Library Cataloguing in Publication Information Available

Library of Congress Cataloging-in-Publication Data

Acker, Victor, 1940-
   The French educator Célestin Freinet (1896-1966): an inquiry into how his ideas
shaped education / Victor Acker.
      p. cm.
   ISBN-13: 978-0-7391-1923-5 (cloth: alk. paper)
   ISBN-10: 0-7391-1923-0 (cloth : alk. paper)
   ISBN-13: 978-0-7391-1924-2 (pbk. : alk. paper)
   ISBN-10: 0-7391-1924-9 (pbk. : alk. paper)
   1. Freinet, Célestin 2. Educators—France—Biography. 3. Education—Philosophy.
I.Title.
   LB775.F762A257 2007
   370.92—dc22
[B]
                                                            2006038900

Printed in the United States of America
♾™ The paper used in this publication meets the minimum requirements of American
National Standard for Information Sciences—Permanence of Paper for Printed Library
Materials, ANSI/NISO Z39.48–1992.

CONTENTS

Foreword

Célestin Freinet, an educational philosopher of the level of Montessori, Piaget, Dewey, Rousseau, and others who inspired entire educational programs, remains quite unknown in the English-speaking world.

Dr. Acker's masterful scholarly study of the 'life and times' of Freinet provides a broad analysis of the French educational perspectives into which Freinet was born, a detailed analysis of the life and experiences of Freinet as he lived through various educational revolutions as well as WWI and WWII, and most importantly, a complete chronological analysis of the works of Freinet that have long laid dormant and untouched in archives across France.

This book is the fruit of Dr. Acker's two-year study of the archival materials of Freinet that are quite spread across France. Supported by grants from the French government, in addition to the current 'historical' study, Dr. Acker produced an earlier 'educational theory' book detailing Freinet's educational theories and their relation to broad educational philosophy. This current study broadens Dr. Acker's study into the tumultuous life and times of Freinet and describes the background of the tumult.

A Chinese curse or blessing is: 'May you be born into interesting times!' Freinet was so mix-blessed and Dr. Acker details the slings and arrows as well as the good fortunes of Freinet. In the previous century the French educational system moved from a 'church dominated' system to a 'government run' system. The transition from a central-authority system to a more democratic system was not smooth with lumps of authoritarianism left everywhere. Freinet sought to eliminate many authoritarian lumps by introducing a 'student centered' seminar-type environment.

Most educational theorists targeted the middle and upper classes in cities, presumably following the money trail. Freinet targeted his reforms across the board, but in particular, at poor and rural educational systems that had almost no resources. He reasoned that any school could afford a printing press since he could buy one himself. And the postal service was universal and cheap. Freinet got most of his lumps by trying to eliminate 'authoritarian' and 'centralized' lumping tendencies in educational systems, the Communist party, the Church, and so on.

Dr. Acker's comments on who did and who did not cooperate with his research and who provided and who withheld documents is illuminating and shows that even today anti-Freinet tendencies abound. Freinet's formal education was limited owing to WWI and the injuries he sustained, but driven as he was, Freinet, always a voracious reader, fitted his ideas into the broad panoply of ideas that have dominated and dogged education through the ages.

Some Freinet scholars have suggested that Freinet's basic ideas were not original with him, and some have even claimed that his main contributions to education were not theoretical or philosophical but merely 'technical'. Freinet brought a printing press into the classrooms of France, and indeed he was not the first, as Dr. Acker points out. Freinet had teachers show students how to use the printing press to produce booklets and printed records of classroom activities, and again, in this he was not the first.

But Freinet was also an educational visionary that saw the printing press as a 'tool' to enable students across many schools to be engaged in an active dialogue by adding 'individual creativity' and 'group interaction' into the process. Freinet undertook to solve the technical problems of coordinating the usage of printing presses in classrooms across France by having the students, in a class, produce materials that could quickly be sent through the postal system to other students in other distant schools to exchange information and perspectives.

Today, using modems, computers and the Internet, our definition of 'quickly' has become abbreviated, and the printing press has given way to the word processor. But these are simply 'technical advances' over Freinet's resources. Freinet's basic ideas carry over almost in toto into the 'modern' communication world.

Freinet developed educational theories and pedagogical techniques for integrating the students of a class with each other, for incorporating the teacher as an 'advisor' rather than as the 'source', and for enabling students to become active agents in the creation and dissemination of information among equals. In reading Freinet's ideas about the dissemination of information among 'peers' written long ago, I was struck by how similar is the wording of the 'scholarly guidelines' of the National Science Foundation, the National Endowment for the Humanities, and other such major granting agencies of the ideas of dissemination of research in scholarly journals and professional communications as well as the concepts of 'peer review.'

Freinet's practical and philosophical ideas, firmly linking 'education' and 'communication,' were far ahead of the ideas expressed by giant government granting agencies/ministries and preceded any inklings of the Internet and e-mail.

What were Freinet's basic ideas about what a school could be? How should students in a class interact with each other, with other students in the school, with the teachers, and most importantly, with other students in other schools across France? Most educators discuss 'the classroom' and the 'classroom dynamics' between the teacher and the students and among the students themselves. But Freinet saw education in a broad social perspective that was 'dynamic' and involved students in a class to directly interact with students in other classes in other schools via mail delivery.

Precisely how did Freinet implement his ideas? To what extent did circumstances force him to modify his theories and technologies? Dr. Acker provides the answers to these and dozens of other questions.

The key element of this book's contribution arises from the author's extensive and rigorous archival searches conducted while living in France for almost two years. The methodology underlying this study required Dr. Acker to search as many archival holdings as possible, and to locate, identify, and verify as many of the original papers from Freinet's extensive corpus of writing as possible. Based on this extensive study of a corpus that exceeds any previously examined, Dr. Acker justifies the claim that Freinet was indeed the forgotten pioneer of not only long-distance learning, but the communical sharing of resources among a broad populace of often impecunious students who were encouraged to think of themselves as an integral part of a 'global seminar'.

Professor Ray Dougherty, Ph.D.
Professor of Linguistics
Department of Linguistics, New York University

Preface

It was in September 1993 that I first heard the name Célestin Freinet. In a graduate course at New York University's School of Education, a professor asked me if I ever heard of Freinet assuming that since I spoke French and was educated in the French educational system, I would know of him. This was not the case! Over the next few years, I became intimately acquainted with the breadth, depth and importance of this man and his work — especially after having spent two stimulating years in France (September 1995–October 1997) as a Bourse Chateaubriand scholar researching Freinet.

The goal of this book is to expand on the most interesting aspects of this educator. It is almost a "how-to" book that will cover the salient aspects of how his pedagogical ideas could be successfully implemented in today's classroom. This book is the second book written to specifically reach English-speaking educators English, and how they could benefit while using a "little bit of Freinet" in their classroom.

This work of love is dedicated to my family who encouraged me and gave me their unwavering support while leading a bi-country life: my mother and sister (Lily Acker and Viviane Levy), my children (Alex and Samantha and their spouses), and my cousins in Fontainebleau (Serge and Mauricette Acker). Most of all, this book is dedicated to my wife, Carole for, without her love and strength, there would be no book.

Finally, once in a very great while there comes along a person, who in life made such an indelible impression upon others by their very being that their memory should never fade: This is the very essence of why I write on Célestin Freinet.

ACKNOWLEDGMENTS

I am dedicating this book to some of my favorite people. . .

• Professor Millard Clements (1924-2005), my mentor at NYU's School of
Education
  • *For always questioning me with a "Why Not?"*
• Jean Chiocchetti (1932-2004), "Mister Grant Man"
  • *For bucking the bureaucracy, and extending my stay in France
  beyond the limits imposed by the Bourse Chateaubriand .* Merci.
• Professor Dennis Sayers, formerly from NYU's School of Education
  • *For introducing me to Célestin Freinet's work*
• Célestin Freinet, whose work and ideas
  • *Have been my inspiration since 1992*
• My family in New York City and Paris
  • *For allowing me to still be "me" far away from home.*
• The friends I met in France while researching Freinet
  •*For opening their homes, hearts, and encouraging me.*

Briarwood, New York
December 2006

Paris, France
September 1995 - October 1997

Chapter 1
Researching Célestin Freinet (1896-1966)

> We aspire to teach men how to live in a democracy, but this democracy is
> not a herd. It cannot survive unless all of us learn how to live it, serve it and
> devote our lives to it.
> — C. Freinet (October 1939)

In his active years, the French educator Célestin Freinet taught elementary
school, developed innovative ideas in education, founded many journals,
created several associations, held yearly conventions for teachers and had
an enduring influence on education in France and other countries within the
international community of professional educators. Besides having written
many books, he also engaged in public controversy concerning the mission,
goals, methods and challenges posed to and by education.

Two major educational initiatives were associated with his life's work:

- Use of the printing press in the classroom
- Interscholastic Exchanges: The exchange of newsletters as well as the
  newspapers written and printed by students.

These initiatives gave the students the impetus to engage in lively classroom
discussions. In today's educational world, these ideas—and more like
them—are the norms and, with the advent of advanced computer
technologies and the Internet, his work is more relevant than ever.

Introduction

Freinet's formative years spanned the tumultuous period from WWI to
the Cold War days following the end of WWII. Recognizing the huge
changes that have taken place since then, one might be tempted to treat
Freinet's as a forgotten historical curiosity, not as a living presence in
the pedagogical world.

Freinet's importance as a pedagogue has been ignored, neglected or overlooked for a very long time, and the contemporary intellectual climate —though captivated by postmodernism—should be encouraged to look into the past in order to be ready for the twenty-first century.

One reason for writing this tome was to give Freinet the voice he did not have. Despite the French philosophical views that time can be divided into neat epochs, it remains that Freinet's voice, long ignored in the English-speaking world, should be heard and updated. We should recognize that his major pedagogical ideas and the depth of their various elements are much needed today to address and redress many pedagogical problems.

This study is concerned with two major ideas that Célestin Freinet wrote about and implemented between 1924 and 1954: *Printing in the Classroom* and the *Interscholastic Exchanges*. Besides teaching and establishing his own school, he wrote close to 3,000 articles in seventeen journals and seventeen books. It is because of Freinet's teaching experience, extensive writing, and hosting of conferences and conventions, that his ideas shaped and changed education in France and influenced educational thought in many parts of the world.

Freinet's journal articles addressed issues in a wide range of periodicals, and were divided in two groups.[1] He was the main contributor to those he founded, and only the contributing editor to the others.

He was a contributing editor to the following ten journals:

• L'École Émancipée (1920-37)
• Clarté (1921-25)
• Notre Arme (1922-35) (Our Tool)
• L'Internationale de l'Enseignement (1923-28)
• Pour l'Ère Nouvelle (1929-39)
• Monde (1929)
• Pédagogie Soviétique (1932-33)
• Le Problème Sexuel (1934)
• Les Humbles (1936-37)
• La Nouvelle Critique (1950)

His contributions to these journals reflect the breadth of his knowledge and various interests. For example, in Berty Albrecht's publication *Le Problème Sexuel*, he wrote a psycho-pedagogical article about an eight-year-old boy masturbating:

Unhealthy sexual curiosity is heightened when children are not given frank, honest and truthful answers about sex by adults (including teachers).[2]

In *Notre Arme*, he discussed how he developed one of his teaching methods, the Interscholastic Exchanges, and he was the founder and editor-in-chief of the following seven journals:

- L'Imprimerie à l'École (1926-32)
- Bibliothèque du Travail (BT)[3] (1932-present)
- L'Éducateur Prolétarien (1933-39)
- L'Éducateur [4] (1939-64)
- Brochure d'Éducation Nouvelle Populaire (BENP) (1937-present)
- Bibliothèque de l'École Moderne (BEM) (1945-present)
- Techniques de Vie (1954-60)

The above list reflects his educational focus. It covers various aspects of the Freinet Technique. Three of the journals he started (*BT, BENP* and *BEM*) are still in existence and are updated, edited, printed and distributed on a regular and worldwide basis by the *PEMF (Publications de l'École Moderne Française)* which was also created by Freinet. Many Freinet practitioners, in and outside of France, still use these updated booklets and brochures for lesson plans, or as additional reference materials.

He wrote about alternative forms of education, which included the use of printing in the classroom and the Interscholastic Exchanges, as well as teaching in rural schools, teachers and teaching, schooling, and life. In his early years, he wrote about political issues of his time:

- The origins of the May 1 celebration (*Clarté*, April 1921)
- Visiting German schools (*L'École Émancipée*, October 1922)
- Visiting Russian schools (*Notre Arme*, October 1925)
- Analyzing Russian pedagogy (*L'École Émancipée*, January 1926)
- Reviewing books with a political slant by Jean Galtier-Boissière, Adolphe Ferrière and Jean Rostand (Edmond Rostand's brother).

Early in life, Freinet espoused left-leaning political ideas and was a strong follower of the pedagogy being developed in post-1917 Russia, whose most ardent proponent was the Ukranian-born Anton Semenovich Makarenko (1888-1939). Much of Freinet's writing was in support of this doctrine.

In late 1926, he started focusing more on his pedagogical vision, and the content and tenor of his writing began reflecting his growing interest in pedagogy and educational methods. In this phase of his intellectual development, most of his writings consisted of articles about:

- Revolutionary ideas in schools
- New types of schools

- Reviewing works by other educators (Piaget, Sanderson, Ferrière, Decroly)
- Printing in school
- Disparaging existing government guidelines.

Most Freinet scholars look for these journal articles because they express his deep-rooted beliefs and thoughts in an unadulterated form. They are a sharp contrast to the more polished version of his ideas found in his books that reflect his wife, Élise Freinet (née Lagier-Bruno) strong editorial influence. She customarily excised and edited some of her husband's rambling and musing.

This author feels that these rambling and homilies found in his journals made Freinet more accessible to his peers. Although his books were more polished, they added very little to our knowledge of him (as a person), and his ideas as a first-rate teacher and communicator. They were his best marketing tools to the outside world.

Freinet was an avid reader of pedagogical literature. Whether it was India's Rabindranath Tagore, England's William Sanderson, Holland's Jan Lightart, France's Paul Robin, or his contacts with other well-known educators of his time (Belgium's Ovide Decroly, and the Swiss trio of Jean Piaget, Pierre Bovet and Adolphe Ferrière). He read and wrote extensively about other educators such as: Jean-Jacques Rousseau, Maria Montessori, Johann Pestalozzi, and John Dewey.

Of the seventeen books Freinet wrote, ten were published while he was alive, and the other seven were published posthumously. Between 1917 and 1940, his life was so tumultuous that he was unable to find time to write. He had plenty of time to reflect while recuperating from being seriously wounded in the 1917 battle of Chemin-des-Dames. This helped him in becoming strongly committed to teaching (1920-40), while fighting his political enemies.

From the onset of WWII in 1939, he was unable to teach, but was able to start six of his books until his incarceration in 1942. After his release from the Chibron camp, he spent the rest of WWII resting at his in-laws' home in Vallouise (High-Alps) while briefly joining the Briançonnais Résistance movement in the Maritime-Alps. There, he completed the books that present his vision of a "modern" education. Those war years were a blessing in disguise as Freinet was able to expand his journal articles, conference speeches and seminars into books.

Early in 1941, the occupying German army closed his school in Vence (Maritime-Alps). After it reopened in October 1946, he was able to finally complete these six books:

• *L'Éducation du Travail*: Students learn by making useful products or providing useful services. It also details proletarian education. It was written in 1942-43, published in 1949, and re-issued by Delachaux-Niestlé in 1960.

• *L'École Moderne Française*: Details the new education, and written in 1943, but did not get published until 1945.

• *Les Dits de Mathieu*: Freinet observed the children in a free environment and discovered the means to develop them by placing them in a milieu that would allow them to expand and grow. It was written in 1946, revised in 1958, and published in 1959.

• *Essai de Psychologie Sensible*: Studies the growth of personality and is based on his beliefs in the *tâtonnement expérimental*.[5] Was published in 1950.

• *L'Apprentissage du Dessin*: It was published in 1950 and explains his inductive and global ideas on drawing. Le *tâtonnement expérimental* is the basis of these ideas.

Five other books followed:

• *Les Genèses* (1953 and 1964): Explains his pedagogy.
• *Le Journal Scolaire* (1957): Details the Interscholastic Exchanges.
• *Méthode Naturelle de Lecture* (1961): Explains his reading method.
• *Les Invariants Pédagogiques* (1964): Details his pedagogical tenets.
• *Essai de Psychologie Sensible* (1966): Updates the 1950 version.

In these books, Freinet explains the beginnings of his pedagogy (*Les Genèses*), details his ideas about the Interscholastic Exchanges (*Le Journal Scolaire*), explains the application of his reading method (*Méthode Naturelle de Lecture*) and ties the Freinet movement to his views on psycho-pedagogy. Élise, and Madeleine (their daughter) edited and published posthumously the following books:

• *Les Techniques Freinet de L'École Moderne Française* (1969): Details the new education in light of many changes.

• *L'Apprentissage de L'Écriture* (1971): Explains his writing method, based on the experimental theory of 'trial and error'.

• *Souvenirs d'Enfance* (1972): Details his childhood memories when he was one year old, and his first years in elementary school.

• *Pour L'École du Peuple* (1977): Detailed a proletarian education.

• *Perspectives d' Éducation Populaire* (1979): Historical approaches to education.

• *Touché* (1996): Details his being wounded in a WWI battle, seeing some of his fellow soldiers die, and narrating his convalescence in a castle. It's a re-issue of the 1927 book.

Souvenirs d'Enfance and *Touché* were about his youth and being wounded during WWI. The other books are philosophical concepts of how Freinet envisioned a 'modern' education.

Besides writing articles and books, he organized and participated in educational conferences. Les Congrès Freinet, started in 1927, were held regularly throughout his lifetime during the school's Easter vacation, but none took place during WWII. At these gatherings, teachers and educators from the Freinet movement in France mingled with their colleagues from all over the world (Japan, Barcelona, Poland, Great Britain, Russia, and Brussels) just to listen and to be inspired by him.

This author interviewed some of those participants who said that, with Freinet's charisma, the seminars were very demanding and intense. Freinet had a very strong sense that he was doing something unique for his students and wanted to make sure that his disciples had the same inner fire as he did. At the end of these seminars, the participants usually left with a renewed sense of purpose, and it kept the impetus of the Freinet movement.

As a corollary to these conventions, Freinet established in 1928 *La Coopérative de l'Éducation Laïque* (CEL)[6] which was responsible for producing and distributing his pedagogical bulletins (*L'Imprimerie à l'école*),[7] his students' newspaper (*La Gerbe*),[8] and the educational 8-mm movies (Pathé-Baby). In 1932, he started a new educational bulletin *Bibliothèque de Travail*(BT),[9] and in 1947, he changed the name of his movement to *L'Institut Coopératif de l'École Moderne* (ICEM)[10] to let the outside world know that he was back from the ravages of war and at the forefront of the figurative battle to modernize the educational system. The BTs, currently used in many schools, are still published by the CEL who also publishes other pedagogical material based on the techniques developed by Freinet.

As teacher, pedagogical thinker, and prolific writer, Freinet energetically addressed the educational and social issues of his day. His importance lies in the substance of his ideas and their influence on education. He also recollected that Leon Tolstoï once said:

The teacher does not like the noise when the children talk, when they move around or when they are happy . . . all necessary activities for their learning. In schools that are built like jails, questions, conversations and movements are forbidden.[11]

Although right-leaning politicians and educators heavily criticized Freinet during his lifetime, he was disillusioned because his peers, the progressive and left-leaning educators, only gave him muted acclaims.

After his death, many of his colleagues expressed the greatness of his work and recognized his achievements. The few eulogies that were published after his death give a sense of his enduring contribution to education. Jean Haccuria's[12] letter to the Belgian publication *L'Éducation Populaire* on October 13, 1966, said:

When WWII started, the pedagogy of the Modern School was very precise and encompassed all of Freinet's domains of education: free expression [*expression libre*], free text [*texte libre*], the printing in the school [*imprimerie à l'école*], freehand drawing [*dessin libre*], engraving on linoleum [*gravure sur linoléum*], free theater [*théatre libre*], current events [*histoire* vivante], and many others. For these and many other accomplishments, we realize that his life as a pioneer was cut down too short.

Haccuria summed up many ideas that were the basis of Freinet's educational revolution and identified the five basic tenets of Freinet's pedagogy,[13] and from Belgium, Jules Goderniaux (Chief school inspector), wrote a letter in the October 31, 1966 issue of *L'Éducation Populaire*, reaffirming that the child was most important in Freinet's pedagogy:

Célestin Freinet has put his stamp on our times. He was the advocate for a pedagogy based on the child, stripped of all sectarian scholastic and highly conscious of a profound pedagogy. Although the late Freinet in his school practiced this liberating pedagogy in Vence, he also had thousands of followers practicing it today, worldwide, in their classrooms.

This apparently revolutionary idea of that time has changed the face and the tenor of pedagogy in France. Today, these ideas are educational principles, which are incorporated into most pedagogical methods. And when Jean Vial, a disciple, a friend and university professor, learned of Freinet's death in October 1966, he wrote[14]:

This movement was an important and an innovative pedagogy affecting our 20th century: some 20,000 teachers in twenty countries . . . Célestin Freinet, my

Master, your fears, your anguishes and your apprehensions were without any foundations: you are among the dead who live intensely. Your work will go on – even without you.

This author interviewed Jean Vial a few months before his death in 1996. In conversation, he expressed his diehard admiration for everything Freinet did, and he remained a faithful friend of Freinet. The above excerpt shows the depth of his esteem and foretells that the Freinet movement will survive the death of its founder.

Professor Louis Meylan, professor of Education and Philosophy at the University of Lausanne (Switzerland), wrote in his eulogy of Freinet[15]:

The most significant pedagogical event of this century (and this is not a hyperbolic eulogy) could have been, but is not, the Montessori or Decroly pedagogy, it is the pedagogy advocated by Freinet. He started with the proletariat school, and other teachers who believed in his credo helped admirably. The Montessori and the Decroly systems are pedagogical systems, while thousands of educators have adapted and used the Freinet techniques to initiate a new life within their students.

Although Professor Meylan merely restated some of Freinet's ideas, he was very emphatic when he said that "*thousands of educators have adapted and used the Freinet techniques to initiate a new life within their students.*"

This was a sharp contrast with the Decroly system which existed only in the Decroly School, located in the affluent suburb of Uccle(Brussels), while the Montessori and the Steiner[16] schools thrived as they appealed to upper-middle class families.

As noted earlier, Freinet's goal was to educate the children of the *working poor*. Early in his career, this pedagogy was very not well received at all because it went against the existing French educational system, which was not responsive to the needs of this class. The educational establishment catered more to the middle class (bourgeoisie) and the upper class, than to the children of the proletariat. This mentality is highlighted in the movie *L'École Buissonnière* when one of the protagonists said, "*The school is an abyss (pit) where the taxpayers lose money.*"

Professor Guy Avanzini,[17] a professor at the Université de Lyon, and the secretary of the Sociéte Binet-Simon, wrote:

Freinet is the only one that has proposed teaching methods that thousands of teachers, in France and abroad, appreciate and use on a daily basis. Not only did he perceive the outdated character of didactism, but he proposed an alternative pedagogy. Also, without really being very explicit on this, his psychological methods to deal with children are quite remarkable as far as the techniques for the adaptation and the readaptation of children at risk.

As president of the École Freinet in Vence, Professor Avanzini, who worked with and knew Freinet very well, continues his work today and remains one of his staunchest advocates. He understood the importance of Freinet's "alternative pedagogy" and fiercely defended it.

In a recent book about Freinet, Professor Patrick Boumard[18] offers another interpretation of Freinet's work and vision:

> We notice that despite the numerous pedagogical upheavals that took place in this century, Freinet was a forerunner, and he remains the major reference point of those who look into the globalization of education. The many educators who had to face dissension, criticism, and exclusion went down the same road taken by Freinet: a road not always paved with roses.

Professor Boumard was quite accurate in his assessment of Freinet, not only because Freinet has affected twentieth century pedagogy, but because he has also changed its dynamics through his tenets of instruction. Every time students in the twenty-first century correspond by e-mail with other students across the room, around the corner or around the world, they take advantage of a method and technique developed by an enlightened educator who once toiled in a run-down smelly classroom in the south of France in 1924.

In 1957, Freinet founded the FIMEM,[19] a worldwide educational association of national and regional movements that bases its pedagogy and cooperative education on Freinet's tenets. It favors contacts and exchanges between teachers and educators engaged in the practice, research, and innovative cooperation based on his pedagogy. UNESCO recognizes the association as a very important non-governmental organization(NGO), and the FIMEM organizes biennial meetings known as RIDEF.[20]

To continue Freinet's work, the association Les Amis de Freinet (Friends of Freinet) was created in 1969, three years after his death, to keep the 'flame alive.' Besides the yearly meeting that takes place in October in its retreat in Préfailles (Brittany), this association publishes a biennial journal with wide distribution in France, Belgium, Italy, Poland, Japan, Spain, Chile and the United States. Most issues carry articles about Freinet, the modernity of Freinet in today's technology-laden world, contributions by former and current followers of Freinet's ideas and very important archival material. As this brief account reveals, Freinet was, and remains, one of the most significant educational thinkers of this century.

Freinet and his Pedagogical Tenets

As a militant teacher and committed educational writer, Célestin Freinet addressed the educational and social issues that affected his students. The issues encompassed problems about class size, the lack of adequate pedagogical material, the rotation of teachers from school to school without consent or their termination without reasons, forcing teachers to abide by antiquated guidelines, and poor working conditions. Here are Freinet's five most important pedagogical tenets:

1. Teachers Are Facilitators in a classroom, not Dictators [21]
Freinet wrote that:

Teachers[22] have an indispensable role to play; they should not monopolize classroom time since students should have a strong voice in classroom life. The platform on which a teacher's desk stood towering over his students should be removed and the desk placed at the same level as his students' desks.

Although Freinet strongly believed that teachers [23] have a vital role in a classroom, he felt that they should not be the only ones speaking in class. Students should have a strong voice in class and should be given the time to express their opinions too. He also wrote that teachers' desks should not tower over the students, but should be placed at the same level as those of the students. Moreover, the placement of students' desks should be configured for the different forms of work, such as a conference hall, a manual workshop, a simple classroom or a reading hall.

Freinet was very much influenced by the elementary school teacher he had when he was five years old. In his book, *Souvenirs d'Enfance*, he said:

The teacher never questioned us about the engravings of the book. The methods of these times were most austere: we read, we recited lessons that no one understood. However, on this day, the teacher made an exception: as a friend, he asked me where the thief's hands were. I knew very well where they were: in our dialect, I would have said that they were attached behind his ass . . . I would have never pronounced before my teacher a word that I believed so coarse. I remained there blushing.

It seemed to me that my pain and predicament were never going to end. Finally, the teacher put an end to my martyrdom by saying: his hands are attached behind his back! I accepted the definition that was far from satisfying to me. However, since the back is not there, I admired the subtlety in using language that knows what to say without shocking.

In another important book, *Essai de Psychologie Sensible*, Freinet talks about this topic using the metaphoric use of "barriers" when he refers to events, people and society affecting pupils in a school environment:

> The school is an all-encompassing environment, but is also an environment that sometimes rejects, puts up barriers, and offers very little help. It is not good enough to tell the families or the schools: Let the children find their own way . . . it is an abnormal attitude . . . We have to guide their lives so that they can climb the various 'floors of life.' But do not be disturbed that one day, they will let go of your helping hand. They will be ready to take their destinies in their own hands. [24]

This important concept for Freinet guided him throughout his career.

2. Classrooms Are Part of the World [25]

Free text [*texte libre*] refers to a compilation of the various texts written by the students; it is in apposition to "text books" [*manuels scolaires*]. Children write about the discoveries in their daily lives and impart this information to others. It is at the core of the Freinet educational method. Correspondent class(es) will receive texts, drawings, manuals and other works of the class.

The creation and implementation of "free texts" were the beginning of the Interscholastic Exchanges,[26] an essential aspect of the Freinet Method.

3. Motivation Makes Students Better Learners [27]

Free texts[28] give children reasons to write well and spell correctly in a precise style. Spelling is not done for itself, but as a necessary tool to convey meaning. By trying to improve a text, students learn rules and discover sentence forms. Although the teachers care for the basic mechanism in writing, free texts are the more important results.

Although Freinet wrote very little on this topic, his sister-in-law, Marie-Louise Lagier-Bruno, wrote two articles [29] in *L'École Émancipée* where she explained the mechanism of the free text and how her famous brother-in-law used it in his pedagogy.

4. Participation of Students in the Classroom Implies Freedom [30]

Freinet's educational method allows children to discover the vastness and the exigencies of freedom as it reduces what is 'forbidden in a classroom.' It allows them to choose a method of working: Either an individual work plan or a collective work plan. Students discover real freedom—one that is not whim or fancy but is engaged in a self-expression.

For Freinet, the interaction in the classroom was a crucial tenet for his teaching method to succeed and for the success of his students in their learning.

5. Participation in the Classroom Nurtures Self-confidence [31]

He sought to make students feel they are capable of progressing, as he was convinced that all children can succeed, albeit in different domains. Some are manually proficient, or skillful orators, or fine writers, and others are good observers. [32]

Freinet saw this tenet as an important one and expressed it as such. Although children schooled in the Freinet Method were conscious of their abilities and were asked to outdo themselves, this method was designed to nurture self-confidence among them, and traditional grading was not used.

Developing these ideas was not a hardship for Freinet since he was an avid reader of the writings of educators in his own country and other nations of the world. His thirst for scholarship, through reading, allowed him to become aware, and he wrote about a plethora of topics:

- Various educators (e.g. Dewey, Ferrière, Montessori, Tagore)
- Physical education (in *L'École Émancipée*, April 1924)
- Modern science (op. cit., February 1925)
- Coeducational teaching (op. cit., December 1926)
- Discipline in the school (op. cit., March 1928)

The Problem

This historical study will closely examine some of the ideas about education in France that Célestin Freinet formulated between 1924 and 1954 and will focus on the origins and development of his ideas about writing, speaking and teaching in which he was engaged. Studying two of Freinet's major contributions to pedagogy in France requires answering these questions:

• What are the Interscholastic Exchanges?
• What were the origins and development of the printing presses?

In this study, we will show how Freinet's work is practiced around the world and how his pedagogical ideas are still implemented today. It will also show that his work continues, long after his death in 1966. This author is positing that it took him time to fully develop his major pedagogical ideas, and that nothing could stop him. Freinet was not ready to end his contribution to teaching children. Answering these questions will enlighten the reader and provide a complete frame of reference for understanding the importance of his pedagogy.

How Significant Are These Questions?

After Freinet developed the use of the printing press in the classroom at the start of the 1924 school year, it became an important pedagogical evolution. Once he witnessed the enthusiasm a snail race could generate among many of his elementary school students, and wrote about it on the blackboard, Freinet realized that, after he erased it, there would be no record of this event in his students' lives.

It got him thinking, *What if the students print their own texts?*, he started exploring the likelihood that, by using a small printing press in his classroom, students would be able to "put on paper" many topics he wanted to teach them. He realized that this method was giving a voice to the students and making him more proactive in the classroom, rather than just being the typical teacher of the 1920s.

A most enduring example of Freinet's influence in today's technology-oriented world, is his development of the Interscholastic Exchanges.[33] In the early 1920s, after he purchased a very basic printing press, which included inks and rubber-backed letters, from the CINUP company, Freinet taught his students how to produce small booklets, and he exchanged them by mail with booklets and newspapers produced by other students in France. The key point is that the students did the work, and he was only their mentor, guide, or facilitator.

Today, many worldwide exchanges are performed either by electronic mail, facsimile or through exchange-student programs. Freinet was very much in favor of the exchange-student program and wrote about it at great length. When he died in 1966, the computer technology was barely there, but it is very conceivable that he envisioned what was going to happen before the end of the twentieth century in France and the rest of the world.

To answer these questions, this author read most Freinet's extensive writings on the Interscholastic Exchanges, and what his collaborators and critics had to say about them. Freinet's numerous articles on this topic were written in these journals and publications:

- L'École Émancipée
- Clarté
- Notre Arme
- L'Éducateur Prolétarien (later known as *L'Éducateur*)
- L'Internationale de l'Enseignement
- Brochure d'Éducation Nouvelle Populaire (BENP)

An in-depth analysis and a study of the Interscholastic Exchanges will explain how this initiative developed, the challenges that Freinet faced in its development and the strategies that he created with his colleagues to promote its use. Since Freinet viewed the extensive use of the Interscholastic Exchanges as a natural extension of printing in the classroom, this was a very significant progression. He wanted to give his students a greater voice than what they had.

Methodology

A key element of this research was the intensive and rigorous archival searches this author conducted while living in France for almost two years. The methodology for this research is based on searching as many archival holdings as possible, identifying Freinet's extensive corpus of writing and using it to justify that Freinet was indeed the forgotten pioneer of long-distance teaching.

What Are Archives?

Documents in archives[34] are normally unpublished records instead of books and periodical publications. Archives are sometimes personal but usually belong to large organizations such as firms and governments; they are distinct from libraries insofar as archives are collections of unique documents whose meaning is derived from their interrelatedness. Nevertheless, a library (or even a museum) can be seen as a sort of archive but the word *archives* is often used when stressing its role of preservation.

Archives were created in the course of conducting public or private business, and all records were not distinguished from library materials and preserved in the same locations as manuscripts. It is only after Gutenberg printed his first book (The Gutenberg Bible) in 1455 that manuscripts were segregated from public records.

The importance accorded to public records has been recognized as one outcome of the 1789 French Revolution. An independent national system of archives was set up to preserve them and, for the first time, the public was given access to them. While archival institutions share with libraries basic obligations to collect, preserve and make material available, they do not select: Their sole function is to preserve organic bodies of documentation, and they must respect the integrity of these documents, maintaining them as long as possible in the order in which they obtained them, cataloguing them and providing research guides.

A distinction has to be drawn between public and private archives. Most countries and states, having recognized the need to preserve their official records, are expected to maintain an archival administration, whose sole purpose is to collect, preserve, and make them available to the public after an appropriate lapse of time. Among the best-known French archival holdings are those of the Archives Nationales in Paris.

The one upon which this author heavily relied was in Nice at the Centre Administratif des Alpes Maritimes (CADAM). Researchers now recognize that non-official archives can have as great a value as libraries. The historical value of their holdings, their preserved manuscripts and similar collections frequently enlightens socioeconomic history. It is also the practice of many institutions (universities, professional and political organizations, secular and religious organizations) to set up their own archive departments.

Location of the Archives

Full answers to the how's and why's of Freinet's Interscholastic Exchanges and the use of the printing press in the classroom necessitated extensive archival search and personal interviews, since Freinet's written word in the field of education was quite extensive and scattered all over France.

This author went through an intense archivist procedure that revealed several unknown elements in Freinet's life. This research project, that lasted more than eighteen months, led to private collections, governmental archival holdings, museums and universities throughout France (Apt, Avignon, Bordeaux, Brest, Gars, Le Mans, Mouans-Sartoux, Nantes, Nice, Paris, Poitiers, Rennes, Rouen, Saillé, Saint-Denis, Toulouse, Vence and Saint-Paul-de-Vence) and outside France (Geneva and Brussels) to find existing and unedited material on Freinet. Additional material was located at New York University's Bobst Library (Tamiment and Wagner Labor Archival holdings).

Besides having searched, selected, acquired and photocopied many documents (letters, articles, educational journals, etc.) from several archival sites, some of the museums visited (Musée Social, Musée de l'Éducation in Paris and Rouen, as well as the Musée Georges-Pompidou—*Le Beaubourg*) yielded additional archival material.

This author interviewed current and former teachers in the Freinet Movement (Guy Avanzini, Michel Barré, Paul Le Bohec, and Pierre Yvin), as well as disciples and educators who knew Freinet (Maurice Pigeon, Henri Portier, Georges Snyders, Emile[35] and Mimi Thomas, Roger Ueberschlag, and Jean Vial[36]). He also interviewed former students from the Freinet schools (Roger Billé), and those opposed to his teaching method—such as Fernand Oury.[37] For balance, assessments were made of books by the authors who influenced Freinet and others who pondered the value of his ideas.

This author lived in France for two years (September 1995 to October 1997) under the aegis of a French Government Research Grant (Bourse Chateaubriand) to carry out an extensive research project on Freinet, based mostly on searching, identifying, analyzing and reading original Freinet material held in various archives.

This author read most of Freinet's books, his extensive educational reviews, trade union journals, communist magazines and leftist publications. This material covered almost a half-century: from an article Freinet wrote in 1920[38] to a letter to his friend Paul Le Bohec, two weeks prior to his death on October 21, 1966. Because Freinet organized conferences for his many followers and sympathizers (1927-66), there was also a plethora of material in this category. A great deal of it was uncovered, although there was a fair amount of material held in private archives that was not accessible for a variety of reasons. Many of the original Freinet followers and adherents had died, others were too sick to sort through their own archival material, or their heirs just discarded the material. In spite of these problems, the Freinet's written corpus and legacy is still staggering.

This author found and was able to obtain unlimited access to study many articles, letters and speeches on or about Freinet. They were held in various sealed archival holdings: CADAM in Nice and the Municipal Archives of Saint-Denis. In other instances, attempts to locate additional archival material were rebuffed: Madeleine Freinet told this author that she was using her private archives to write her father's biography and what it was to live with a genius father who stunted her growth, and attempts to get access to the French communist party (PCF) archives were met with a resounding **NYET!**

In order to access the French government archives, a special dispensation to the "French Privacy Law on Official Documents" was obtained from the ministry of Culture. It gave this author permission to read, photocopy and quote material found in sealed archival documents, letters, and magazine articles concerning Freinet. This archival search became the basis of a historical study that relied on historical research but this author formed his own opinions solely based on critical thinking and editing existing material on or by Freinet.

What Is a Historical Study?

A historical study describes both the past and what is written about the past. It defines history as being the "past experience" of society. The concern of the historian is to make available to society that past experience and record it for future reference. The historian reconstructs events from trails and indices, selecting those relevant to the task, and establishing relationships that would allow a varying freedom of choice by the historian. It also introduces the subjective element of the historian's personality that cannot be eliminated from historical writing, but the historian's aim is to make the margin of intellectual error as small as possible.

The methodology of history (historiography) does not radically differ from other disciplines. It also searches for existing knowledge, new and relevant data, creates hypotheses, and as in all historical writing, success depends on skill and experience. Division of the past on temporal or topical lines merely reflects the human limitation and the skill of these historians.

As a Freinet historian, this author could not experience the occurrences themselves since all that was available were accounts of occurrences as seen by his contemporaries or archival material. In the study of Freinet, a historian's eye was used to find the answers to the questions this author posed—relying almost exclusively on archival material.

Interscholastic Exchanges: Texts Written and Printed by Students

An analysis will be made of Freinet's writings on the Interscholastic Exchanges, and very early in his teaching career, he attempted to create an exchange program among teachers. As Secretary of the Maritime-Alps' Teachers' Union, he was also the education expert for its magazine *Notre Arme*, and called this approach "Les Cahiers Roulants" (rolling notebooks).

As interesting as it sounded, he quickly abandoned this idea because it focused more on the teachers and did not involve the students.

Monsieur Primas, the teacher from Villeurbanne (a suburb of Lyon), was the first to have his students print their own texts and exchange them with Freinet's students. The Interscholastic Exchanges really took off when René Daniel became Freinet's most serious correspondent in October 1926.

This elementary school teacher from Trégunc-St-Philibert (Brittany), expressed an interest in exchanging, on a regular basis, the bulletins that his students printed with those printed by Freinet's students. Daniel, like Freinet, was dedicated to the welfare of his students, and active in the teachers' trade union and politics. They exchanged regularly printed texts, postcards and locally-produced food and non-food items. After Freinet started his first successful interscholastic exchange with Daniel, he wrote:

> As of June 1926, the idea to connect our two classes is excellent. I have already trained my students to use the printing press. Can we start this October [1926] exchanging journals between our two schools?

By January 1927, the exchanges became more personalized since each student was assigned a specific correspondent. By December 1927, there were twelve different schools, and the exchanges took place several ways. Another important aspect of this pedagogical idea—and key to Freinet's Interscholastic Exchanges[39]—was the exchange he established with other schools: exchanging newspapers or booklets printed by his students, "cultural packets," or teaching material with other teachers.

In May 1929, two of Freinet's colleagues tried to launch a summer exchange-student program, but there is no known documentation on the success or failure of this program, save for a 1947 article written in BENP by two of the teachers who had a successful program during the summer of that year. By the time Freinet felt the program was working well, there were at least forty more articles written on this topic in these journals:

- Notre Arme
- L'Imprimerie à L'École
- L'Éducateur Prolétarien, and L'Éducateur
- L'École Émancipée
- L'Internationale de l'Enseignement
- BENP
- Fédération Unitaire de l'Enseignement

These exchanges were wholeheartedly endorsed, accepted by most Freinet adherents, successful and beneficial. In today's advanced technology world, we use fax machines, Internet, electronic mail in addition to regular mail.

It is important not to lose sight of the fact that Freinet was an avid reader although he missed the opportunity to complete his formal teacher-training program due to WWI. While recovering in the hospital from his war wounds, he used the free time to read. This is an essential observation since Freinet was always looking for innovative teaching methods to make up for not completing his formal teacher's education.

Origins and Development of the Printing Press

An analysis will be made of the writings about printing presses written by Freinet. He wrote his first article on this topic in *Clarté* of June 1925, and the last one in *L'Éducateur* of December 1939. Altogether, there were fifty-five articles written on the uses of the printing press in the classrooms. Freinet wrote most of these articles in these journals:

- Clarté
- Pour L'Ère Nouvelle
- L'École Émancipée
- L'Éducateur Prolétarien and L'Éducateur
- L'Imprimerie à l'École
- L'Internationale de l'Enseignement
- Monde
- Fédération Unitaire de l'Enseignement
- BENP

In December 1926, Freinet's book, *L'Imprimerie à l'École*, detailed his ideas and how they would benefit his students. He collaborated with Lucienne Balesse[40] on the last known article he wrote on the topic of *Reading through printing in the classroom* (la lecture par l'imprimerie à l'école) in the n° 7 issue of *BEM*, published in 1961. Four articles also praised printing in the classroom as a major pedagogical tool:

- Eugène Villermoz. "À L'École de Gutenberg." *Le Temps*. July 4, 1926
- J. Aicard. "L'imprimerie à l'école." *Notre Arme*. February 1927
- Ad. Ferrière. "L'imprimerie à l'école primaire." *Pour L'Ère Nouvelle*. March 1927
- G. Barré. "Chez l'inventeur de l'imprimerie à l'école." *L'École Bernoise/ Berner Shulblatt*. November 1938.

Other educators associated with the Freinet Movement wrote after his death in 1966 important articles that still questioned his method:

• Pierre Guérin and Eric Debarbieux. "From printing in school to the printer."[41] *L'Éducateur*. May 1987
• Claude Guihaumé. "Les origines de 'L'Imprimerie à l'École':1926-30." Bulletin de la Société d'Agriculture de la Sarthe.1991

The material on hand from the extensive archival search yielded sufficient material to validate the importance of these research questions. Printing in the classroom, as part of the Freinet Technique, was not such a revolutionary idea. In 1718, the printer Jacques Collombat[42] taught the future King Louis XV to print while studying.

Likewise, Freinet saw it as a necessary tool to raise the level of the school. On the front page of the July 4, 1926, issue of the influential newspaper *Le Temps*, its editor, Villermoz, wrote an article, *À L'École de Gutenberg*,[43] in which he applauded Freinet and clearly agreed that his judicious use of printing in the classroom was quite significant:

This psychologist (Freinet) noticed that the child feels a strong and lasting bond with his ideas when he sees them printed. It also gives the committed teacher an excellent tool to reach his students.

After the teacher purchases the basic equipment (a 'hand-press', ink, paper and recycled lead print characters), the students can see a blank sheet of paper become alive with their thoughts, the narration of interesting events, or the research they carried out. This process validates them as individuals and validates their teacher's experiments. Like all wordsmith, the students must choose the correct words carefully and respectfully since many readers respect and are in awe of the power of the printed word.

Other newspapers (*Clarté, Le petit Niçois*) and the Italian newspaper (*Il Corriere de la Sera*) noted their respect for Freinet's significant pedagogical ideas.

Conclusion

Each of these ideas will be studied in the following chapters. In chapter 2, the author will describe the genesis of how Freinet founded and used printing in his classroom, and the impact it had on his disciples and on many educators in and out of France. In subsequent chapters, the author will describe how the use of the *Interscholastic Exchanges* was a natural extension of *printing in the classrooms*.

The author will also analyze Freinet's vision of how these exchanges were beneficial to educating his students and how students worldwide today are benefitting from these ideas. Freinet's influence and contribution to education were mostly felt during the tumultuous era between WWI and WWII, when political, philosophical, and educational turbulence were common, and he was an easy target for his disparagers and enemies. As an innovator, this was the credo that Freinet tried to uphold throughout his life.

NOTES

1. In brackets are the years of his contribution
2. All French texts and expressions translated by the author.
3. The BT's are a series of practical workbooks/classroom teaching material.
4. Same as above, but Freinet changed its name to mollify the Vichy government.
5. Tâtonnement expérimental = experimental theory of 'trial and error'.
6. CEL = *Coopérative de l'Éducation Laïque* = Cooperative of lay teaching.
7. L'Imprimerie à l'École = printing in school, started in 1926.
8. La Gerbe = the sheaf.
9. BT = *Bibliothèque de Travail* = library of work (more than 300 bulletins exist).
10. ICEM *(Institut Coopératif de l'École Moderne)* = Cooperative Institute of the Modern School.
11. Tolstoi, *The Complete Works of L. N. Tolstoi*, pp. 164-172, Vol.VIII.
12. Inspector of schools in Brussels.
13. These tenets were explained in this chapter.
14. Vial, Jean. "L'École et la Vie." *Freinet: Mon maître.* 5 novembre 1966.
15. *Éducateur et bulletin corporatif.* "*Hommage à C. Freinet (1896-1966).*" N° 39. 11 novembre 1966. Montreux (Suisse).
16. Based on the Rudolf Steiner's pedagogy.
17. Société Binet-Simon. *Célestin Freinet (1896-1966).* N° 493. Décembre 1966.
18. Boumard, P. *Célestin Freinet.* PUF. Paris. 1996.
19. Fédération Internationale des Mouvements de l'École Moderne = International federation of the modern school movements.
20. Rencontres Internationales des Éducateurs Freinet = International meetings of the Freinet educators.
21. Plus de dictature du maître.
22. Freinet, Célestin. *Essai de Psychologie Sensible.* Delachaux & Niestlé. Suisse. 1966.
23. Ibid.
24. In: *Essai de Psychologie Sensible.* pp. 133-134.
25. La classe fait partie de l'univers.
26. C. Freinet & S. Carmilet. "Correspondance interscolaire." *L'Éducateur.* N° 4. p. 58-59. 15 novembre 1945.
27. Intense motivation de l'activité à l'école.
28. Freinet, Célestin. "Le texte libre." *L'Éducateur.* N° 6. 15 décembre 1946.

29. Lagier-Bruno, M-L. "Vie Pédagogique: La rédaction libre à l'école primaire." *L'École Émancipée*. N° 29. p.470-1. 15 avril 1928 & N° 30. p.487-8. 22 avril 1928.

30. Participation signifie liberté.

31. Participer c'est acquérir une confiance en soi.

32. Freinet, Célestin."La Technique Freinet." *BENP*. N° 1. Septembre 1937.

33. C. Freinet & H. Alziary. "Les correspondances scolaires." *BENP*. № 32. Novembre 1947.

34. As defined in: *http://www.en.wikipedia.org/wiki/Archives*

35. Émile Thomas died in 2003, in Brest (Brittany).

36. Jean Vial died in Paris in 1996, from Parkinson's Disease.

37. Fernand Oury died in Paris in 1999.

38. Freinet, Célestin."Chacun sa pierre: capitalisme de culture." *L'École Émancipée*. N° 35. p. 134. 22 mai 1920.

39. Known as: *Correspondance* or *échanges interscolaires*.

40. Lucienne Balesse, from Brussels, was a trusted colleague of Freinet.

41. De l'imprimerie à l'imprimante.

42. Collombat's influence on Freinet as detailed in J. Gonnet's dissertation: "Les journaux produits par les jeunes en age scolaire." Université de Bordeaux III. 1985."

43. At the Gutenberg school.

Chapter 2
Freinet and the Interscholastic Exchanges

Contrary to beliefs held by many French educators and specialists about the life and times of Freinet, the idea that Freinet was the sole creator of the Interscholastic Exchanges—the necessary companion to the school journals —is erroneous. In this author's other book,[1] he debunked the myth of originality in Freinet's work and showed that he copiously "inspired himself," borrowed or gleaned from a great variety of learned sources and incorporated many in his pedagogical method known as La Technique/Les Méthodes Freinet.

This study was not undertaken to diminish him. *Au contraire*, it was undertaken as a tribute to his greatness, the breadth and depth of his knowledge, as well as his uncanny ability to select and cull ideas from ancient and current educators. With all this material in place, Freinet was able to transform them into a coherent pedagogical "tour de force." Moreover, it was done from material and ideas that were "out there."

Freinet's Sources to the Interscholastic Exchanges

As a result of this author's extensive research conducted in France (September 1995 to April 1997), it avers that three educators had a major influence on Freinet on the topic of Interscholastic Exchanges: Ferdinand Buisson, Paul Robin and Ovide Decroly.

Ferdinand Buisson and the 1882 *Dictionnaire Pédagogique*

One of the first texts written on the use of Interscholastic Exchanges in a classroom setting was in the *Dictionnaire Pédagogique* (Pedagogical Dictionary), edited by the former Minister of Education Ferdinand-Édouard Buisson.

Buisson's genius was not in the writing of the various entries but in his ability to choose enlightened educators capable to sum up the status of the various aspects of culture and education in a simple yet erudite manner. Buisson (1841-1932), a well-known educator, reorganized the French primary school system, and as National Director of Elementary Education (1879-96), assisted Premier Jules Ferry in drafting statutes that took the public schools out from under the church's control (1881 and 1886) and made primary education free yet compulsory (1882).

He also was a founder of the *Dictionnaire Pédagogique*, of which the 1882 edition is considered the finest. In 1898, Buisson helped found the Ligue des Droits de l'Homme (League of Human Rights). As president of this organization (1913-26), his peacemaking efforts—during WWI and his postwar work for Franco-German amity—earned him the 1927 Nobel Peace Prize, along with Ludwig Quidde (1858-1941), a German pacifist.

H. Métivier, an inspector of academy and close collaborator of Buisson, wrote the following entry on Interscholastic Exchanges in the 1882 *Dictionnaire Pédagogique* more than forty years before Freinet ascribed his ideas on the same topic:

> The goal set by the teachers who organized la correspondance scolaire was to help their students express themselves correctly by exchanging their ideas with other students in writing. Some teachers, either spontaneously or under the advice of enlightened school inspectors, organized an exchange of letters between their students and other students in their own schools, on either topics provided by facts of school life, or facts suggested by other teachers.

> The students read the letters received by each classroom aloud, with comments from the teacher, and corrected, if necessary. The teacher's role is to elicit, without showing it, the corrections that have to be made. The responsibility to respond to this letter is given to one student or a group of students chosen by the teacher. The work in a group is far superior since it integrates several children in a task that they enjoy and where the emulation is active.

> For the school correspondence to work well, it is important that the teacher neither help his pupils, nor correct their letters. We found that the critical mind, so difficult to awaken and to develop in children from rural areas, and so necessary to enlighten among city children, works better when it is time to criticize other people's work than one's own. It is true for everybody: Children, adults, or famous scientists.

> The teacher's abstaining in the writing of these letters is also vital to the success of this endeavor. If the children do not have the deep conviction that this work is their own work and that no one is cheating, they will not have the same ardor anymore. Conflicts between teachers and students will erupt, and in the end the school correspondence would be doomed.

In two departments[2] (Ardennes and Pas-de-Calais), they have organized this correspondence between schools from the same district, and between distant schools (neighboring district or department). It works well because there is a strong commonality of ideas that allows the young correspondents to broaden their horizons, their ideas and their intellectual domain.

To organize the correspondence between distant schools, teachers might want to ask their respective school inspectors to help. It would also have the advantage of using these inspectors as a resource since they will be aware of all other school correspondence programs, which could be beneficial to one school or another.

Keeping this exercise in tight reins is necessary, making sure that it does not become too absorbing and hinder the regular teaching. For example, a letter per week will be sufficient: one letter received and one sent. The choice of topics could become difficult, and the teachers must be very ingenious. They could inspire themselves from various incidents of school life, a visit by the inspector, the vicar, or even by the mayor. Moreover, other activities such as installing a new wall map, opening of a school library, facts of the life of the village or the city, elections, serious but a real accident, the crop, a description of the village, explanation of the village's unusual custom, in fact anything that requires attention and observation.

Let us develop the faculty of observation in our children: to know how to watch, to understand and to explain objects or facts is a precious science that can never be lost; so many people do not know how to watch! Why not let the exchanges generated by the school correspondence include girls too. Girls have a quicker and nimbler mind than the minds of young boys, and if their self-esteem gets hurt in the process, at least the distance considerably lessens the danger of serious injuries, as the contact is an impersonal one.

In summary, the school correspondence is an excellent stimulant to start new ideas and develops those that are already in progress. It is also a way of learning how to express ideas, deal in a courteous manner, and form the critical minds of schoolchildren, while giving them a more attractive method for learning theories and lessons in grammar and composition. One major drawback to avoid would be to make sure that the emulation does not degenerate into a nefarious rivalry of unhealthy self-esteem, or that teachers use this technique for self-aggrandizement.

For the school correspondence to work, it must remain spontaneous, naïve, sincere, and to be an exceptional intellectually recreational activity rather than normal and all-too frequent school exercises.

Because Freinet was such an avid reader, he amassed an inordinate amount of knowledge in the pedagogic field. Métivier's article in *Le Dictionnaire Pédagogique* was a resource that definitely made an impact on him.

Others who Influenced Freinet: Paul Robin and Ovide Decroly

Besides having read Buisson's dictionary, Freinet also read *Cempuis* by Gabriel Giroud who detailed Paul Robin's "integral education" and the usage of printing in his Prévost orphanage. He also admired Decroly, whose students at The L'Ermitage School in Brussels used printing as a pedagogical tool.

Who Was Paul Robin (1837-1912)?

Robin, born in a middle-class family from Toulon,[3] entered the teaching profession in 1864. He dedicated himself to teaching the masses. While teaching in a high school in Brest, he attempted to introduce "school walks[4]." A year later (1865), unable to live under the imperial regime of Napoléon III, Robin left for Belgium. There, he joined the Belgian branch of the International Workers' Association (IWA) in Brussels where he gave free lessons to poor families and signed manifestos favoring strikes. He was expelled for his political ideas and took refuge in Switzerland.

In Basel, Robin took part in the 1869 Fourth Congress of the IWA. When he returned to Paris in 1870, he was still the secretary of the association, and on June 22, 1870, he was condemned, along with thirty other militants, to two months of jail for being an adherent in a secret society. He was freed on September 4, 1870.

Unable to enter Paris during the Commune Uprising, and conscious of his complete political impotence, Robin took refuge in London, and he remained there until 1879. He befriended Karl Marx but did not agree with his authoritarianism, being a strong believer in individual liberty and autonomy . . . the signature trait of anarchists, not communists.

Upon his return to France in 1880, Robin was named director of the Orphanage Prévost in Cempuis. It was founded by a bequest, and the General Council of the Seine[5] ran it as an orphanage and a school. It was neither a "new school in the country" nor a state-run institution, but an institution in which the state had the wisdom—for a very short time—to put "the right man in the right place," which was rare.

Unfortunately, this admirable orphanage lasted only fourteen years (1880-94). During that time, Robin gave his knowledge, his undying energy, and all of himself to build stone by stone his work and his legacy. And because Robin was misunderstood, scoffed at and the butt of attacks from the clerics who could not tolerate his humanistic approach to teaching—which was more simplistic than dangerous—he reaped no outward glory.

The knowledge that he had done his duty, the justifiable conviction that he had done pioneer work, sustained him to the end . . . and then he was fired. Followers of obscurantism—an attitude that opposes reason and progress to an irrational fear of learning—hounded him so much that he committed suicide in 1912.

Robin's Pedagogical Tenets

Paul Robin, concerned with both theory and practice, practiced it through his integral education.[6] His method allowed each child to continue to work out his development according to circumstances, needs, and personal initiative.

Boys and girls were enrolled at the school in Cempuis— and this went against educational practices of the times where most schools were segregated. As everywhere, when carried out under good conditions, it proved to be an element of moral health, joy and rivalry in work. In 1880, this coeducation worked unusually well in a residence that held as many as 200 students.

In spite of the usual insinuations by overzealous clerics, no serious negative facts were uncovered to spoil this system of education. Life at Cempuis was very active and interesting: the children were educated in a family-like environment, and the Catholic Church never condemned coeducation in a family. Gabriel Giroud wrote:

> What impressed visitors to Cempuis and the people who lived there, were the happy faces, the animation, the clear eyes, and frank bearing of the boys and girls attesting to the perfect serenity of their conduct.[7]

At Cempuis, the household maintenance and domestic chores (beds, laundry, general cleaning of the house) were in the pupils' hands. The older ones helped the younger, and they carried out—as fully as possible—all the aspects of practical hygiene. Excursions and trips lasting several days were frequent and had a definite goal:

> The students visit a shop, a factory, local workshops and continue to frequent them regularly, to the extent of an hour and a half daily. The

sight of a spectacle of nature, of a spring, a valley, a historic or prehistoric monument, a living lesson in science, geography, history, and morals remains part of their daily activities.[8]

Like Freinet, Paul Robin also advocated a well-rounded education:

All the children at Cempuis without exception, boys and girls, shared in the manual work since it gave them a sense of being skilled with hand and eye. These skills could be used later in their apprenticeship to any manual trade rather than making them begin in their early years a specialized apprenticeship to a particular trade.

In accordance with a rotation so arranged that all the children may visit all the shops, each one 'butterflies'[9] successively for periods of about a month through this series of shops from his eighth to his eleventh year, at which time most of them move on into the upper classes. In these classes, the students do manual work in the shops for three hours a day, and continue butterflying up until their twelfth year.

These 'butterflying' activities were diverse. The students chose them in consideration of their own preference and aptitudes, with the competent assistance and advice of the master-workman, the teachers, the directors, and the pupils' parents or guardians. Among these: printing, stereotyping, electrotyping, lithography, zincography, photography, bookbinding and book boarding, framing, typewriting, etc.

Some of these shops, the print-shop for example, took orders from the outside, and their work was so well liked that it became necessary, in order not to overload the students, to send part of the orders to another shop. Boys and girls alike shared in these various activities to a degree commensurate with their powers. After the 'butterflying' was over, specialization came in to separate the sexes on the basis of their respective capacities, it was deemed advisable for the girls to know how to carry on men's occupations at need, and for the boys to know enough of household affairs to be able later on to take their wives' place on occasion.[10]

And from the standpoint of formal studies:

The part played by the occasional, irregular lesson, which can be given in class, but equally well out of class, anywhere, at anytime, but a mere outline, not prepared in advance, improvised, given when any object comes unexpectedly to the children's attention so as to make the most of the occasion; in constant use, it is the happiest auxiliary of the teaching.[11]

In the teaching at Cempuis, a constant appeal was made to "quickness of eye, skill of hand, to the spirit of inventiveness." In arithmetic, the pupils counted, tallied, weighed, measured; they compared lengths, magnitudes and time-intervals.[12] They also performed various meteorological observations.[13]

Reading and writing were taught at the same time. As to writing, an original idea employed at Cempuis was to teach stenography to children at a very early age.[14] Fundamentally, stenography is to writing as the Esperanto language is to one's mother tongue, and the idea of inculcating the universal elements of grammar by means of a language which throws them into relief is not so strange as it may seem at first thought. Incidentally, Freinet was a proponent of Esperanto as a teaching tool.

For relaxation and liberty, Robin set aside three hours a day for *optional work*. He explained the reasons for this practice:

> This last point appeared to me to be extremely important. It corresponds to children's free hours at home. It is then that the educator can study the tastes of the children, and can encourage or modify them. It is then that the pupils can develop their taste for sciences, trades, various achievements, and to devote themselves freely and fully to whatever particular interests they might have: Photography, painting, sculpture, music.[15]

It is a pity that the example set by the Prévost Orphanage was isolated and has never been imitated elsewhere. This brilliant Frenchman launched ideas, but did not maintain or promote them; he was quick to jump to conclusions, and rarely adopted other people's ideas. He would have needed an indomitable will and a few valuable partners to overcome the inherent trouble linked to this innovative pedagogy.

For Robin, an education was not a neutral state, but decidedly internationalist, pacifist and proletarian. It was especially debasing that his ideas were the true motives for his scandalous and unjustified firing.

Paul Robin, apostle of this popular and liberating teaching, aimed to make Cempuis a high-energy center and his soapbox to introduce a new education. For several years, educators from all over France and surrounding countries met in Cempuis to study the system of education that Robin advocated. These educational meetings were exhilarating, but unfortunately the accounts of these conferences are hopelessly untraceable.

Who Was Ovide Decroly (1871-1932)?

Doctor Decroly was a pioneer in the education of handicapped and normal children. He was a physician who became involved in a school for abnormal children and consequently became interested in education.

Because of this interest, he established in 1901 the *Institute for Abnormal Children* in Uccle, a wealthy suburb of Brussels, a school that provided a homelike atmosphere for these children, and where Decroly obtained better and more consistent learning results than many schools for normal children were able to achieve. Its success prompted Decroly in 1907 to open the École de L'Ermitage, a school for normal children on whom he further applied his methods.

Viewing the classroom as a workshop, Decroly based his curriculum on analyzing the children's needs within four important categories: food, shelter, defense and work. Their needs were at the center of a year's study and, within the framework of their needs, were encouraged to develop their individual interests. His program became known as the *Decroly Method*.

Decroly's Pedagogical Tenets

Decroly sets forth the characteristics of his program and justifies them in the following terms:

> The school must fulfill its general educational goal by preparing the child for real social life, and this preparation is best provided for when the children are introduced practically to life itself in general and to social life in particular.

> This introduction to the material of the program necessitates the examination of the two fundamental fields of knowledge. One is the knowledge by the child of his own personality, the power of self-knowledge and consequently of his needs, aspirations, aims, and ideals. The other one is the knowledge of the conditions of the natural and human environment in which he lives, on which he depends, and upon which he must act. With the realization of these needs, aspirations, aims and ideals, mankind will be able to progress, to cooperate in this process, and to have a conscious, intelligent sense of solidarity.[16]

Decroly was a strong believer in making the children become self-sufficient individuals by developing the knowledge of their own needs:

Endeavoring to confine ourselves to facts easily observed by the child and to facts which have the widest repercussion on human activity, we distinguish those essential needs:
- The need for food
- The need for protection from cold, bad weather, and others
- The need for self-protection against the various dangers and enemies
- The need for cooperation, recreation and self-improvement
- The need for light, rest, association, solidarity, and mutual aid
- The knowledge of the environment: human environment (society, family, school), living (animal), vegetable, and solar (sun and stars) to satisfy the needs.[17]

Decroly's Influence on Freinet

In trying to link Freinet to Decroly, this author encountered an ambiguous situation and faced a daunting task. It seems to be difficult to attribute some of Decroly's pedagogical innovations and ideas to what Freinet used in his classrooms and his books, but it is relatively easier to point out the ideas culled from the other educators since it was previously posited that Freinet liberally used them in creating and defining his Freinet Technique. This author strongly believes that Freinet was uncomfortable "liberally copying" from someone (Decroly) who was still alive at the time (1924-31). He was making his mark in education, while many other educators were long gone . . . and possibly forgotten!

While Freinet adapted, perfected, and popularized many of Decroly's ideas that he incorporated into his technique, he felt there was a limit to Decroly's contribution. He was a strong defender of the rigid applications of Decroly's pedagogy. While he emphasized Decroly's dynamic contributions, defended his word, and credited him without feeling the need to establish a rational lineage from his pedagogy to that of Decroly, he was strongly opposed to the propensity that kept on comparing him with or putting him in apposition to Decroly.

He did not want to be placed in the same rank as Decroly; he felt he was on a different and higher level. To some extent, there was an obvious continuity between Freinet and Decroly: Freinet's manuels scolaires (school manuals) are the texts of the first *Livre de Vie* (Book of Life) that his students printed; they are very close to what Decroly established in his school. Freinet called this printing "making a long detour in the opera called life" to discover what every good child psychologist come across in a child: Common sense and life.

In fact, this is how Decroly prioritized his work: First of all, he was a medical doctor, second a child educator and being an educator was third.

Freinet placed many caveats in the paths of those who compared him with Decroly. For example, Decroly's implementation of the printing in the classroom was completely different from what Freinet did. It is an easy temptation to which one is invited to not succumb since there are less applicable and pertinent ideas than it seems. But for those who insisted on uniting them, the quest for analogies and dissimilarities that they presented somehow alleviated the relative inconsistencies that they offered.

Decroly and Freinet lived in a twentieth century Europe that faced secularism, capitalism, democracy, the first extended crises of the industrial era, the development of a new statute for children, the development of studies of the unconscious and the effort to look at mankind in a more scientific manner. These educators, belonging to the Pantheon of Education whose thoughts were considered radical, were now considered pioneers in the history of education and lauded for their persistence in wanting those changes. Decroly and Freinet shared similar longings.

They studied, experimented and applied innovative teaching and training techniques that did not rest any longer on the concept of the child as a small object, something that man could mold and randomly fill with arbitrary ideas. They instituted a pedagogy using specific topics, and they endowed their pedagogy with its own dynamism based on knowing and respecting children, thus enabling the youngsters to grow as autonomous individuals.

All children are similar and different and these methods were a much-needed departure from the accepted norms of their time. Freinet and Decroly were cognizant of these differences. They responded appropriately as far as prevention or remedy is concerned, and adapted their methods to suit the children surrounding them.

Decroly and Freinet—each in his own way—instituted a successful pedagogy from which no child would be excluded and no child would be left behind. Both of their ideas faced mounds of incomprehension and intense resistance. Those who judged their ideas and enterprises for being detrimental to society and reducing the influence of bureaucracy did not peer far enough into the future: Decroly and Freinet were the future.

Although their educational ideas were similar, they also differed considerably. The two educators were influenced by the different centuries in which they grew up: Decroly was mostly a nineteenth century person, while Freinet was most definitely a twentieth century person. Everything about them was different, from their socioeconomic and cultural backgrounds, their years of formation and profession, domestic lives, beliefs and political involvement, speech, to their concepts about education. All these were very distinguishing traits.

Thus, the innovation was born, and Freinet, as a teacher, was confronted with the difficulties of teaching in a popular and proletarian milieu. As a practitioner and researcher, Freinet was anxious to observe, to establish an efficient didactic method and to fully educate.

He was a strong believer that, even if confused, he was certain to achieve that through experimental 'trial and error.' On the other hand, Decroly—a scientist, a medical doctor and a psychiatrist—became a teacher to help children with all types of nervous disorders. He dedicated himself to surveying and adapting these children. Coming across these exceptional children in the hospitals of Brussels was decisive.

As a medical-pedagogue and researcher-practitioner, Decroly was a scientist who studied maladjusted as well as normal children, bringing together scientific investigations and applications into the creation of a school for the life of his youngsters. To advance his research, Decroly recruited and trained collaborators and hoped they would contribute to eventually improve his work.

Unlike Decroly, Freinet who created the CEL in 1928 to serve the people, he opened it to all the teachers interested in his ideas and how to teach them. Freinet remarked:

> We radically distinguish ourselves from the educational movements that preceded us, since it is without doubt the first time in the history of the pedagogy that an action for renovating really started from scratch. We are a crucible of ideas for this movement of 'new' education.

The fact remains that Decroly and Freinet were situated as rivals and placed on an equal footing, and certainly, their coming together could satisfy the old-fashioned impulse of comparing and copying. It is worth considering that Decroly and Freinet paved the ways that we need to boldly borrow in order to build a more just, wiser and more scholarly community. Although Freinet was familiar with work done by Robin and Decroly, and gleaned some of their ideas, he was still searching for something different.

An Idea Developing in Freinet's Fertile Mind

Freinet came back from WWI as a tired and grievously wounded young man with ambivalent feelings toward teaching. Under the minister of education's imposed rules and regulations, he felt he didn't have the stamina to teach under the constraints of such conditions, and for his own sake, he had to change the ways he taught.

In October 1920, he was assigned to teach at the elementary school of Bar-sur-Loup.[18] After the 1920 teachers' convention in Bordeaux, his third piece in *L'École Émancipée* stated that:

> The International Teachers' Union, created by teachers interested in a new education, is against wars and hate, and will keep a vigilant eye on pedagogic literature – especially schoolbooks and books for young people. Our group will give directions to the different groups and we will have our own journal (written in Esperanto) and a center for Interscholastic Exchanges for teachers and students.[19]

Although this is the first time Freinet mentioned the exchanges, he was already aware of what they were from his reading about them in Buisson's Dictionary, which he read while convalescing. Seventeen months later, he brings up again this subject in an article written in *L'École Émancipée* of March 1922:

> Although Soviet Russia instituted free postage for the interscholastic exchanges, my German correspondent Heinrich Siemss told me that he could only write to me infrequently because mailing a letter in Germany is very high, and that their currency has been devalued[20]. . . But the fact remains that international correspondence between workers (meaning the teachers) is becoming harder.[21]

Freinet was ready to burst on the scene with new and revolutionary ideas.

Freinet's First Exchanges: Les Cahiers Roulants

As the secretary of the Maritime-Alps' Teachers' Union, Freinet was the education expert for their magazine *Notre Arme* and wanted to experiment with a different approach to school correspondence. He called it *Les Cahiers Roulants*.

It is important to remember that Freinet missed the opportunity to complete the necessary formal teacher-training program due to the onset of WWI. As an avid reader, he used his free time—while convalescing in the hospital, or at Gars—for reading and analyzing innovative teaching methods to make up for not completing a formal teacher-training program.

As a result, Freinet became a great believer in what he called *le tâtonnement expérimental*, as it mirrored his own search, but before the Interscholastic Exchanges were fully functional, Freinet toyed and experimented with the idea of teachers exchanging postcards with other teachers. Louis Spinelli, the secretary of the Teachers' Union urged Freinet —in one of his first contributions in *Notre Arme*—to organize the teachers:

> At the request of Freinet, the Union Council has decided to organize an exchange of educational postcards. Send maps and cards to Freinet, teacher at Bar-sur-Loup.

In the February-March 1923 issue of *Notre Arme*, the following article is decidedly a precursor to the school correspondence, and Freinet considered using the rolling notebooks in his Bar-sur-Loup school. Freinet wrote:

> Many of our young colleagues are often faced with the embarrassing situation of not being able to find interesting and well-written recitations that they can adapt to their classrooms. Good compilations exist, but one is required to know and buy them, and these choices are rarely satisfying. It depends on us to constitute the choice of our dream.

> We are circulating, as of today, a notebook in every circumscription. We ask our colleagues to write down various pieces of prose or poetry that might be the most interesting and the best adaptable for their classroom, those that their various students liked the most. After completing it, address the notebook to your colleague in the neighboring town so that he can appraise and choose what might interest him. Write down his name and address on the first page to facilitate the roll-out as well as the copied pieces.

> We have indicated the general order for the circulation of these rolling books on the first page, but it is not mandatory. We ask the very last colleague of this roll-out to return the notebook to me: Célestin Freinet, at Bar-sur-Loup.

> When this first round of rolling is completed, we will consider the means to make all our colleagues benefit from our collaborative effort. We appeal to your good will so that the notebook be returned to the secretariat at your earliest convenience. When you are finished fully with the notebook, please attach it to another notebook, or to additional pages.[22]

In the educational section of the June 1923 issue of *Notre Arme*, there was yet another article by Freinet discussing the rolling notebooks:

> I feared that these rolling notebooks had gotten lost, buried under piles of other notebooks, victims of this inertia that hinders all our projects. And voilà! The notebook from Grasse comes back to me complete, with

supplementary pages, after having circulated in Bar-sur-Loup and Coursegoules, and gone through the hands of about twenty colleagues.

This is a very encouraging result: About forty recitations for the different courses, constituting an interesting and promising choice. I hurriedly copied some of this poetry for my own students, and sent back notebooks 1 and 2 toward Grasse. I am hoping that other areas enjoyed the same success, but with the summer vacation fast approaching and notebooks not having finished their circuit, I am asking the colleagues that have them then send back them to me. We will put them back in circulation in October (1923).

A few months later, in the February 24, 1924 issue of *Notre Arme*, there was this brief paragraph by Freinet:

We ask the rolling notebook holders to either circulate them, or return them to Freinet at Bar-sur-Loup, if they are filled. (s) Freinet.

This was the last time *Les Cahiers Roulants* were mentioned in *Notre Arme* or any other publication. Even the usage of the postcards fell by the wayside. Thirty-four years later, in the October 15, 1958, issue of *L'Éducateur*, Freinet briefly noted in the article that these cahiers roulants were his first attempt at establishing a school correspondence.

This author believes that Freinet gave up this experiment because it gave the teachers an important role and excluded the students. In the Decroly's school, the teachers printed while the students watched, but Freinet wanted his students—as young as possible—to get their hands dirty with black ink and learn by doing. This correspondence, coupled with the printing, was born in Freinet's mind, with the help and the unwavering support of many educators and his family.

The Interscholastic Exchanges: The Freinet Way

Freinet was less than pleased with the feeble attempt of exchanging postcards with other teachers, and was not enthused on how Decroly's and Robin's implemented printing in the classrooms, since these teachers got their hands dirty, not the students.

Freinet decided that it was pedagogically very sound to have the students "blacken their hands with printing ink," print their own work, bind it, illustrate it, and send it to other schools and correspondents across France. To him, the successful completion of this cycle from concept to completion validated his pedagogy.

In October 1925[23] Freinet started printing in his classroom. It seems that one of the earliest references Freinet made about the Interscholastic Exchanges was found in the June 1925 issue of *Clarté*.[24] Although words such as Interscholastic Exchanges or "school correspondence" are not specifically mentioned, this is what he had to say:

> Leave the official schoolbooks behind and let the students live. They come in this Monday morning, highly spirited and their eyes full of the sudden storm that has bleached yesterday the countryside with hail.

> Will we still cover the science lesson proposed for this day? Definitely not. We give them ways to be ready to write down observations. They write a text and we all read it with enthusiasm because it is text based on a live event. A group of three or four students writes it in fifteen or twenty minutes while—the teacher who does not interfere—sees the other students continue their work: individual reading, arithmetic exercises, mostly studying according to a method close to self-teaching.

> After the composition is finished, they print. With a rudimentary hand press, they quickly print 100 sheets in five to ten minutes. Each student inserts a copy in his *Book of Life*. They will be sending thirty-five copies to their schoolmates at the school of J and forty for those at the school of F.[25]

> At 10:00 a.m., the mailman appears with packages from the schools of J and of F. You can imagine very well the relish with which our students devour the writings of their comrades who live so far away, in areas they cannot place on the map, yet they learn the main thing that interests them: how other children live. Don't you think this is a very rich tapestry for reading?

> They are not reading fictitious or uninteresting material. It is about the lives of our young students. Not only does the printing of the texts in the classroom make possible the realization of this life, but I would like to see that those who will read these lines could manage to live the intense life I have been living for the past six months (December 1924) in my renewed classroom environment.

In the July 4, 1926 issue of *L'École Émancipée*, Freinet talked about some of the first Interscholastic Exchanges[26] he carried out with the teacher Primas from the elementary school in Villeurbanne, and this is what he had to say:

> The use of our material printed in the classroom became the unexpected source of an interesting activity in our public schools: I want to speak about

the exchange of printed material between several French and foreign schools. During the school year (September 1925-June 1926), we regularly exchanged our printed material with Mr. Primas' class, and this exchange offered an infinity of advantages:

1. Interest for a class to follow the life of another class.
2. Initiation to the diversity of the world through the display of an activity.
3. Topics studied in another school are most likely different from ours.
4. Exchanging city plans, postcards or other documents helps the study of geography.
5. The goal of the written composition is even more precise because the printed material is not only read in our class, but in a distant class, which makes the students fear their judgement.
6. The students's writing must be interesting, clear, precise, clean, etc.
7. Without textbooks, the students read much more. This year, thanks to our two *Books of Lives*, they read more than 3,000 lines of text, the equivalent of a 200-page book.

Although I measure the quantity, the quality of the texts and work, the incomparable virtue of these printed sheets is that they are alive and felt by the writers, that they fully understand them, and that this experiment was a revelation for me. It brought me many joys and very pleasant surprises.

My students never ceased being interested in it, and strangely enough, no one refused to compose, ink, illustrate or work on printing. They considered this work as a favor I am doing for them and they are always interested. Finally, because of the many requests for information, approvals and encouragements that come to me from all over the world, this is proof that this experiment was latent in the mind of many of my colleagues; they are happy to test its actualization today.

In October 1926, at least six other European schools will start working with printing works and the exchange will be far more interesting. It would be even more interesting if other colleagues joined us to develop this experiment in all directions.

In his in-house bulletin, Freinet detailed his views on how the Interscholastic Exchanges should proceed with only seven or eight of his faithful adherents:

This exchange must be carried out as regularly as possible. Your classroom must deliver a sufficient number of printed papers, meaning a number slightly higher than the number of students in the corresponding classrooms. These printed papers must have texts perfectly correct, printed very clearly, and cleanly. It is essential that these conditions be met and we meet these expectations with hard work. Get in touch with the teachers from the corresponding schools for your mutual needs and goals. You can subsequently exchange postcards, manuscripts, etc. Your printed material could be shipped as *Printed Material* after you obtain the permission from your postmaster for such a reduced tariff.

Remember that the most important material to print is about the real life of your students – in and out of their classroom. It is something which will interest these young students more. I believe that one daily exchange is enough for now as it makes an average printing of 80-90 sheets, more than enough. Thus, you can begin this exchange as of the first days of class and continue it, even if some colleagues are late in sending their contributions.[27]

However, in a different issue of the same publication,[28] he was more forceful in discussing the impact of the exchanges:

In spite of the rudimentary conditions of collaboration to the first number, the launching of 'La Gerbe' was a success, although the paper was of bad quality, and had disparate form and texture. Cutting up the sheets anew was necessary; the enthusiasm and the ingeniousness of the collaborators countered these imperfections. This first issue was so well received by the students that we had to produce more than double the expected normal amount (180 copies). This encouraged us to improve since *La Gerbe* represents for us:

1. A tool to improve teaching: The emulation between classes is certain. In our next issue, each school must do a much better job of presenting their work and their centers of interest. This school journal will be pleasant, instructive and will feature interesting reading. It will be one reading most appreciated by the children because it features work of other children. It will bring invaluable contributions to the various other productions by young children.

2. A stimulant for the technical improvement of printing and exchanging: For the next month (May 1927), each collaborator will receive a certain number of free pages to be printed for the revue. Good quality paper, a more convenient format and simple illustrations (on wood or linoleum) will help the students to produce beautiful pages.

3. An invaluable means of propaganda for printing: It has taken place in the class room and the interscholastic exchanges. With a goal to make known our technique, I will talk to the comrades who have requested additional copies of 'La Gerbe' and try to convince them to join our initiative.

4. A feature of closeness between the schools: It will be shown by supplementing the exchanges with additional items (locally produced food or artisanal items).

In the June 19, 1927 issue of *L'École Émancipée*, Freinet addressed the concerns of a larger audience of educators interested in these Exchanges:

> One of our colleagues believes it is useful to remind his comrades that need and usefulness are the main ideas behind the school correspondence. We are not talking about correspondence by mail considering the high cost of stamps, but a regular correspondence using our experience of printing in the classroom. In this way, we would achieve the perfect goals of teaching: the need to speak properly, to practice writing composition, to read interesting texts, and to learn about life, geography, and working conditions in other countries, etc. Thanks to printing our work, these Interscholastic Exchanges can be performed at a very low price because we can send printed material at an extremely low cost.

> Our group has greatly expanded and the Interscholastic Exchanges have become very popular now. Personally, we have put in place an exchange with our comrade René Daniel that is of great interest to us and gives us many teaching advantages. This exchange is wonderful and the two Books of Life we gained would certainly convince many teachers to take up printing and exchanging the product of their printing with other schools.

> We perform a regular exchange (every other day) with a school and a twice-a-month exchange of all our printed material supplements it with 20 schools. If you want interesting reading, we receive many of them every two weeks from our correspondents. One of the achievements we can be very proud of is the creation of a cohesion and an emulation between the classes that work with their printing words. What we do is considerably richer than a simple exchange of letters.

Freinet added:

> I do not regard printing in the classroom as a panacea. I do not cease to describe that printing in the classroom is not a method, but a technique, a tool that each of us employs as it suits us as teachers, and to the best interest of our schools.

> Let us keep in mind that by distributing this tool, we make it a more invaluable teaching tool, and it might even help us get rid of all the bad schoolbooks and the sellers of these books. Hopefully, this will pave the way to a new education and more progressive.[29]

By December 1927, Freinet was able to formalize his ideas about the Interscholastic Exchanges, and explained them better in *L'Imprimerie à L'École*:

Our group increased so dramatically this year that doing a simple exchange of our semi-monthly newspapers between us is no longer possible. It became necessary to organize teams. We have agreed upon the following regulation:

1. We have divided the members into teams of 12 classes of identical levels, so that the exchanges produce the maximum pedagogical impact. At their request, the schools with several levels of a given grade can form several teams.
2. All the classes must take part in a mandatory, semi-monthly exchange. Additionally, each class can also carry out personal correspondence with other classes, if it wishes.
3. We form the teams so they can function the whole school year.
4. When new teams adhere late, we pair them with an existing team, until they can become part of a team. The members of the existing teams help the provisional members service their newspapers.
5. Each team collaborates at publishing a special 'La Gerbe,' with a special binding by one member. To maintain a perfect connection in this endeavor, we invite all the members to send a copy of their newspaper to Freinet who will be the overseer. He will not correct any of your newspapers!
6. Because of the high cost of postage, we did not include schools and correspondents in foreign countries in the teams's make. Those of you who wish to correspond with them can do it directly.
7. This is a minimum regulation that is necessary for all the members to conform. If a class cannot, even temporarily, ensure a service of regular exchange, it must inform its fellow members and partly compensate by sending letters, postcards, etc., if it wishes to keep its rights of correspondence.[30]

Freinet was on his way. He felt that this method seemed to work and that most of his adherents were very enthusiastic about it.

Basis for the Interscholastic Exchanges: The School Journal

Freinet believed that in order for the Interscholastic Exchanges to work efficiently and permanently, they must be based on the school journal. Later in this chapter, we will see what necessary qualities a newspaper must have to prove it is an excellent tool for exchanging ideas. First, let us look at its technical realization.

The Real Journal Scolaire Must Be Printed

Freinet emphasized this aspect not to elevate himself, but because it was really the best way to display his students' achievements. Printing gives the newspaper an aura of being a serious endeavor, thus lending credence and success to this technique:
    1. Among the graphic techniques of the 1920s, only printing allowed a perfectly legible black text to make a good impression and leave its mark on the readers
    2. Everything else considered, Freinet was the first to recognize that the printed newspaper spontaneously attracted the children in the classrooms; they often refused to read stenciled pages, even if the texts were quite interesting
    3. Most of the schools that experimented and exchanged "printed matters" were clearly in favor of producing and exchanging a "real" newspaper.

The School Newspaper Will Be Illustrated

Freinet experimented with various rudimentary methods of illustrating texts printed by his students. Because the authorities did not recognize the value of his pedagogy, Freinet had to experiment with limited available resources and settled on engraving on linoleum to produce illustrations.

    The children, those who were particularly talented and interested in images, drew and engraved on the linoleum and enhanced their drawings with colors. All other considerations taken into account, children tend to go first toward illustrated newspapers, and, more particularly, to those that they have colored themselves.

The Freinet Technique In The Classroom

Since many schools did not own a printing press, Freinet recommended that they could use instead two basic and rudimentary printing devices, similar to a stencil: the *nardigraphe* and *limographe*. Both techniques, if used with dexterity by the teacher, could produce a decent-looking newspaper, even if it would not be very colorful and rather expensive.

Let us note that Freinet was never fond of stencil printing and rarely recommended its use since the few papers that used that method were almost illegible and not very well accepted by young readers.

Producing a newspaper with handwritten manuscripts or with stencil papers was, at best, a stopgap method that Freinet very reluctantly accepted or recommended. He felt that the necessary extensive input of the teachers and the resulting poor output would discourage the students from participating and disillusion the teachers.

The Proper Printing Procedure

Freinet asked five or six of his students, known for having the most legible handwriting, to copy the free texts displayed on the blackboard on special notebooks. After they produced pages for the newspaper, others enhanced the pages with color or illustrations; the students enjoyed reading those newspapers especially when comparing them with the other poorly printed newspapers.

Nevertheless, to Freinet, it was not enough to just print a newspaper. It must be printed neatly and legibly so that the juxtaposition of texts and illustrations would stimulate the interest of parents and correspondents, in addition to the students.

By the mid-1930s, after almost fifteen years of developing and working on this technique, Freinet felt that he had accomplished a lot to achieve a well-produced school newspaper. Not only had he developed and perfected the printing press to simplify its use, but he also gave a great deal of instruction to improve the output.

Although Freinet was very pleased by the quality of the newspapers produced by many of his followers, he always reminded them—particularly the beginners—that it was not the quantity of material that counted in a newspaper, but the quality.

Many teachers did not want to omit material composed by the students and crammed as much as they could on each page. It resulted in airless, cluttered and illegible pages; but when blank spaces, illustrations and texts are strategically juxtaposed, the effect soothed the spirit and encouraged the students, parents, friends and correspondents to read, enjoy and respond to their work. He said:

A newspaper page should be as close as possible to a masterpiece. To achieve this goal, there is the need for a concerted effort between the students and their teachers to produce a newspaper with judicious layout, well-placed blank spaces, interesting drawings and clarity in the printing. It is hoped that when the correspondents will receive it, they will say, 'Ah, this looks very nice!' even before reading it, and 'This was an interesting paper' after they finished reading it.

Major newspaper publishers know that adults and children react to skillfully printed headlines in bold black with inserted pictures—that aerate and lighten up the text—even if some of them may not be relevant to the text:

> Pay the utmost attention to these observations in the editing and printing of your newspapers. Be sure to use good quality newsprint and mostly maintain regularity and punctuality as far as publication date is concerned.
>
> Let your paper come out on the same date at the end of the month. Don't delay it eight to ten days on the pretense that the study that began is not finished. You can continue it in the following number. What is indispensable today is to publish the paper, even in a slimmer edition. You will complete it, if necessary in the following chapter.[31]

Regulating The Exchanges

Freinet did not just organize the correspondence from class to class by simply exchanging letters or documents in a very haphazard manner such as "The School of X would like to correspond with a school in Region Y." He wanted it more formalized.

Although this type of haphazard exchange would have some advantages, he felt that due to the lack of proper tools, method and support, it would not create a pedagogical advantage or generate the positive enthusiasm obtained by implementing the Freinet Technique.

He advised the teachers interested in printing and exchanging, to start with a handwritten school newspaper to awaken the interest of their students. Once this step was achieved, they will be more interested! With this indispensable tool firmly in place, the school newspaper was ready to roll. Freinet would make available his help, resources and services.

Schools wanting to participate in these exchanges were incorporated into teams of four, six or eight classes. The organization of these teams was a delicate endeavor since it was based on the needs of the schools, the various grades and their interests. Also, all these schools—whether in rural areas, in the mountains, near the shore, in the North, in the South or in the center of France—expressed a preference for schools they wanted to be paired with and why.

Freinet requested from the schools interested in this service to fill a correspondence questionnaire. From the information provided, he attempted to pair off the schools to the best of his ability. Additionally, he gave each school the latitude to correspond with other schools of their choice or with a second team.

Because Freinet remembered the fumbling and difficulties he encountered in his first year, he wanted to publish a directory of schools interested in publishing. He instituted a team system to help some of the schools that received more applications than they anticipated and were unable to fulfill all the requests for exchanges. Most other schools attempted to maintain a reasonable schedule of correspondence since it was a basic component of their pedagogy. This is what he said on this topic:

> In the second year of school, you and your students will be able to ask for and keep some of your old and faithful correspondents over and above the new team in which you have been integrated. While attending conventions and training seminars, or performing exchanges in a haphazard manner, you will become acquainted with new comrades who will become your quasi-permanent correspondents.[32]

Freinet's adherents understood and accepted that, to be successful, the Interscholastic Exchanges had to be carried out in two ways: monthly or regular exchanges. Although the schools were scattered throughout France, each class was obligated to perform a monthly exchange of its school newspaper with other classes assigned to its team.

On a weekly basis, each class edited and printed its texts or drawings for itself and for each of its corresponding schools (ten to twelve copies) and kept them in a special file until the month's end. Then all the printed sheets were gathered into a newspaper, with the school's identifying cover and mailed out. The work entailed in preparing this material was educational. To that effect, schools that were dedicated and well organized designated students who would be responsible for facilitating the automatic exchanges. Those students would prepare mailing labels and send newspapers, documents or packages to schools when advised to do so. Additionally, they would be the first to receive, file and read newspapers sent in by other schools.

Freinet felt very strongly that the monthly exchange—considered a little too impersonal, even when supplemented by additional letters or packages to maintain intimacy—was not sufficient to show the advantages of the permanent enthusiasm derived from this technique. He thought that the students were short-changed on a personal level because these exchanges did not afford them the time to know themselves and their correspondents better.

Freinet devised a secondary type of exchange, the regular correspondence, in which selected students from various schools were nominated as *regular correspondents*. These students would immediately contact the teacher of any given school to find out the number of pupils in a class, the setup of the class, and, as soon as possible, the students' names and ages.

Freinet saw that the letters exchanged between students were uneven in quality and content. For example, many letters written by 13- and 14-year-old boys, not his students, but some of the other teachers' students, were subjective and did not fully describe their lives. He also felt that their illustrations and presentations did live up to the standards he set up for the other schools to follow and did not become boring material to the young readers. He recommended:

> The school with whom you correspond has twenty-seven pupils, yours has twenty-four. You have ten monthly correspondents, and want to dispose of twenty newspapers to accommodate the subscribers. Therefore, your daily printing will be 27 + 24 + 10 + 20 for a total of 81 copies.

> After one page is printed on both sides – for your students who take their book – we recommend the use of our invisible see-through binders, which permit children to make up, day-by-day, a real 'book' which at the end of the year will be quite imposing. You perforate the printed pages and give one to each pupil. After individual reading either silently or aloud (children like to re-read the text clearly), the page is added to the book. This diary (*Book of Life*) will get twelve stenciled pages, drawings or even pictures to thicken and enrich it.

> We prepare twenty-seven sheets, which we put in envelopes and mail to our corresponding school. They receive our package and distribute one sheet to each student. They read the texts in silence or aloud, comments are made as well as explanations given, notes are taken of their reactions and questions or answers are prepared; each student places the sheet received in a second *Book of Life*, the one from the corresponding school. Each student will have two books: One from his school and the other from the corresponding school; they are diaries which complement each other marvelously.[33]

Below is a very simple example of these exchanges, from the teacher Suzanne Carmillet[34] of Tlemcen, Algeria:

> One day, in my Second Grade classroom of 40 students, two of my young girls bring various texts on the Festival of The Sheep, and we very enthusiastically decide to prepare a document regarding the last night of Ramadan (known in Arabic as Eid El Kebir) to send to our correspondent

in France. Quickly, in teams of two, the students divided the assignment: they wrote down what they knew, researched and questioned their parents and other elders on what they are unaware of. They filled out informational cards on the following subjects:

- Origins of the Festival
- Purchase of the sheep and its arrival at the house
- Slaughtering the sheep and the Festival
- Washing the sheep's fleece
- Use of the meat and preparing the couscous
- Various other dishes prepared on this occasion
- Drying and storing the sheep's meat.

On the assigned day, each team presented the results of their research in front of an engrossed audience. After the students did all the necessary corrections, they carefully recopied their work, illustrated on cardboard the product of their research, put on a simple binding, added a colorful cover and voila . . . their work was ready to be sent. As the teacher, what was my cost? Negligible. I directed their work a little, and spent some of my personal time investigating the same thing they were investigating to make sure of its accuracy. I also got to know my students better![35]

That's exactly what Freinet wanted his followers to do. Thus devised, it was an example of how the correspondence stopped being impersonal as these daily texts brought echoes of their private lives, and the students and their teachers got to acquaint themselves with the other students as if they were nearby.

They completed this exchange by regularly sending letters to their correspondents. For example, every fortnight each student wrote to his best friend: *Mon cher ami* (camarade), and enclosed pictures, stamps, and other personal mementoes with his letter.

After the teacher would read these letters—having previously explained to them that he reads their letters not to censor them or check their grammar or spelling, but to avoid potential trouble—they were mailed in packages, accompanied by a cover letter from the teacher to his correspondent with any pertinent explanations concerning this mailing. Freinet depicted a class receiving such a package:

You should see the excitement in the classroom when they receive this mailing. Interest is at its highest. Each child receives his correspondent's letter as a treasure; he puts it away neatly, takes it home and guards it preciously. There's no problem to that; it may happen that some pupils will not receive any answer to their letter because the correspondent is sick and has not written. This brings about real despair, which shows us the value these pupils attach to these exchanges. It will also be necessary for the teachers to arrange something between themselves to avoid recurrence of such mishaps at any cost, even if it means asking some pupils to write a supplementary letter to be sent to those kids who were not receiving any mail.

The parents are very much interested in these exchanges and at times correspond between themselves. It is worth mentioning the numerous advantages that our school derives from the integration of this technique in the life of the family and of the village. Every month, our Bar-sur-Loup school prepares a package for our correspondents; each pupil brings a small package for his particular correspondent with his name and address.

What does he put inside? Newspapers, pictures, toys, photos, a knife, valuable presents. In these special packages, our mailing consists of a communal share: Chestnuts, nuts, marbles, almonds, oranges, potatoes, which can be enjoyed by everybody. The package is solemnly mailed, the mailing should be done by the pupils who will (mentally) follow its route and will anxiously await to hear of the reactions.

The arrival of these packages raises in an indescribable enthusiasm our classes. No other pedagogical event equals the animation this one brings about. One must have lived through such moments to understand such affirmation. Unforgettable scenes! After twenty years, I still remember having received from René Daniel, our correspondent from Trégunc, a parcel containing "crêpes bretonnes"[36] thin as muslin and deliciously buttered. The distribution was made: Three pancakes to each kid, and the teacher was included. You should have seen the joy of each child taking home to their brothers or parents the remainder of their small part! At night, the kids came back saying, 'My father said we must send them oranges, figs.'

One day, a parcel arrived from a school in the Ardèche[37] containing a batch of chestnuts, which were quickly put on the stove to roast. On another day, the young students in the Freinet School received sweets and two bottles of Champagne January, from their Marne correspondents. Reims, capital of the Marne area, is the world's largest producer of Champagne.

With such response, the teachers quickly realized the impact of the correspondence and the element of life it brought to the work in the classroom. The correspondence also motivated many classroom activities.

When the students wrote, they thought of their correspondents. When they inquired about history, or arithmetic, they informed them. When they described their village or region, with maps to validate their description, they executed a perfect job since they responded to inquiries or requests from their long-distance friends.

All these considerations greatly influenced the schoolwork itself, since the students were willing to put their best foot forward. It also affected their choice of free texts while better focusing their centers of interest to fulfill the goals. Freinet's teaching did not give much credence to intellectual theories of learning but was rather centered around work and life, which are both important keys to his pedagogy.

Pedagogical Advantages of the Interscholastic Exchanges

Freinet had an almost messianic faith and a deep sense that the advantages of the exchanges were considerable and would be greatly appreciated. He felt that the pedagogical advances and the advantages offered by this method were among the best preparations he could offer tomorrow's generation. He saw three distinct pedagogical advantages when the usage of the Interscholastic Exchanges became the mainstay in the classroom:

1. From the emotional to the functional:
The neophyte teachers will be curious and infatuated by the novelty of this method. Their emotions will prevail when they receive exchanges, but this euphoria will abate and will be replaced by a more functional attitude. That is when the exchanges will be integrated in their everyday lives. Their preoccupation with learning, knowing, answering and corresponding will affect the way they teach and interact with their students. With older students, there will be acceptance in light of the expanse and importance of the works. The middle-grade students, after having expressed their doubts, let this new-fangled method settle in and accept it. Finally, for the very young students and those "special students," their emotions might get in the way of accepting, understanding or participating in these exchanges.

2. The exchanges inspire the expression:
An everyday occurrence between teacher and student when they meet in the morning is the student saying,*Monsieur, Monsieur, I can write a nice story for my friend Pierre in Albi,*[38] and the conversation starts since the teacher naturally wants to know about it. The shape of speech thus started, prepared and achieved, the written expression is destined for the correspondent. The pupil will unfurl all his talent and effort to show off to far-away comrades, and he will express himself by writing and drawing for his peers. It is not a formal activity but rather a functional one. He doesn't accomplish an exercise or fulfill a task; he is part of an exploration and

frees himself for others. This functional activity takes all sorts of shapes according to temperaments, circumstances, needs and reactions. The inquiries that are asked for, or offered, necessitate all the key elements of the exchanges: Writing, graphics and material. Writing produces the most natural and most indestructible activity for children.

3. The Interscholastic Exchanges As Source of Documents:
    This method will enable the schools to stretch the framework of their investigations. Since all the classes in the groups have varied and numerous correspondents, each one in each newspaper must add a page in his *Book of Life*, something based on a local event with a precise documentation on that subject. If each school receives ten sheets of historical documentation from ten classrooms throughout France (e.g., Brittany, the Rhine Valley, Lille and the North, or the Pyrénées), monthly during the ten-month school year, they will have received 100 documents of uncontested value. The creation of this page of history offers many advantages. It allows the creation of a large amount of rich documentation with constant progress. It motivates the search for subjects, thereby leading the class to action toward the desired goal.
    The comparison of the various environments gives rise to curiosity. Here is what our comrades have found. Is there something similar with us? The question of these exchanges and this brotherly help may lead to a big development. We hope to see the formation at the heart of our group, resolute and active groups as to the work history, directed in a cooperative manner, forever and more complete.

Conclusion

The experiment that Freinet carried out in France, its main elements which have been described, is fairly conclusive. Therefore, since all this is known, it presupposes an organization of a communal life and a cooperative for which the school journal is both the cement and the fruit. Freinet offered the following caveat to the educators:

> Scholastic will kill you; you are fed up with teaching lessons and correcting homework and no life for you and your family. Your students are weary of you as much as you are weary of them. The school journal and the interscholastic exchanges bring a practical approach–which seems to be officially recognized–to break the yoke and to lift your arms toward the sun, the work and your life.

It is this cooperative life that is difficult to attain. Unless the teachers get inspiration from the technical exchange that has just been detailed above, they will not attain modernization and success—which are their goals.

NOTES

1. Acker, Victor. *Célestin Freinet*. Greenwood Press. July 2000.

2. In France, a *département* is similar to a state, but smaller.

3. Toulon: major sea port on the Mediterranean Sea.

4. The school teacher takes his students on exploration walks around their neighborhood.

5. General Council of the Seine: It is a group of elected officials from an area surrounding Paris.

6. Giroud, Gabriel, Cempuis. p. xv.

7. Ibid. p. 33.

8. Ibid. p. 59

9. Translated from the French word "butiner," which means "to hop from flower to flower, while collecting the pollen or the honey."

10. Ibid. p. 91.

11. Ibid. pp. 118-19.

12. Ibid. pp. 123-24.

13. Ibid. pp. 125-27.

14. Ibid. pp. 148-150.

15. Ibid. p. 280.

16. Ovide Decroly & Gérard Boon. *Vers l'École Rénovée*. Bruxelles. 1921.

17. Mme. E. Flayol. *Le Dr. O. Decroly, Éducateur*. pp. 79–100. F. Nathan. Paris. 1934.

18. A small village in the Maritime-Alps, located 14 miles from Cannes.

19. Freinet, Célestin. "Vie Pédagogique: L'Internationale de l'Enseignement. Pour la révolution à l'école."*L'École Émancipée*. N°. 4. p. 15. 23 octobre 1920.

20. This was due to the economic hardship that Germany felt following the 1918 Versailles Treaty ending WWI. These harsh conditions fueled the rise of Fascism, Nazism and Hitler.

21. Freinet, Célestin."Vie Sociale: Une autre forme de la réaction." *L'École Émancipée*. No. 24. 11 mars 1922.

22. Freinet, Célestin. "Échanges de cartes postales." *Notre Arme*. Février-mars 1923.

23. The "official" date for ascertaining Freinet's start of the printing and the interscholastic exchanges is not very accurate because Freinet had a tendency to mix dates and events. His journal writings are, in all probabilities, a more accurate repository of his chronology.

24. Freinet, Célestin. "Vers l'École du prolétariat. Contre un enseignement livresque:l'imprimerie à l'École." *Clarté*. No. 75. pp. 259-261. Juin 1925.

25. Although not officially identified by Freinet, J is the team headed by the teacher Jayot in Carignan (Ardennes) 180 miles N.E. of Paris, and F is the team headed by the teacher Faure in Grenoble, 345 miles S.E. of Paris.

26. Freinet, Célestin. "Vie scolaire: L'imprimerie à l'école." *L'École Émancipée*.No. 40. pp. 593-95. 4 juillet 1926.

27. Freinet, Célestin." Circulaire aux adhérents." *L'Imprimerie à l'École*. No. 2. Décembre 1926.

28. Freinet, Célestin. "La Gerbe." *L'Imprimerie à l'École*. Bulletin No. 4. Avril 1927.

29. Freinet, Célestin. Vie Pédagogique: La correspondance interscolaire réalisée par l'imprimerie à l'École. *L'École Émancipée*.No. 38. 19 juin 1927.

30. Freinet, Célestin. "L'organisation des échanges." *L'Imprimerie à l'École*. Bulletin No. 9. Décembre 1927.

31.In *Le Journal Scolaire*. p. 33.

32. Freinet, C. et H. Alziary. "Les correspondances interscolaires." *BENP*. No. 32. p. 7. Novembre 1947.

33. Ibid. pp. 7-8.

34. She was the school mistress for girls.

35. Ibid. pp. 58-59.

36. Thin pancakes from Brittany neatly folded.

37. Ardèche is an area located in the center of France.

38. Albi is a small town in the Pyrénées, 440 miles south of Paris.

Chapter 3
Printing In The Classroom

Children have strong feelings when they see their thoughts printed, they feel pride and dignity when they see their words in print. Printing gives life to their words!
"À L'École de Gutenberg", *Le Temps*. July 4,1926

Although Freinet died in 1966, his legacy did not die with him. It is still palpable today and is more vibrant than ever. When Freinet started more than eighty years ago, his Interscholastic Exchanges with René Daniel of Trégunc-Saint-Philibert, from his one-room schoolhouse in Bar-sur-Loup (Maritime-Alps), this author is quite sure that he did not anticipate that millions of students, teachers and parents in many countries would owe him a debt of gratitude. He was only devising an innovative pedagogical method to suit the needs of his proletarian students. Freinet said:

> The dream of all the modern educators who are looking for a rational education is to make the life of a child and the life of the village the center of the life in the classroom. The necessity to teach reading from textbooks conceived, written, and printed by adults cannot be implemented to meet the needs of our students and their milieu. But if we have a printing device that would allow us to print what interests us, and if our students can put down on a page their thoughts, their feelings and narratives they wrote, then these pages become the centerpiece of their schoolwork.

> Additionally, if we can establish regular exchanges with other schools that also print in their classrooms, then all of our students can probably widen their horizon, and greatly expand their knowledge. With these two pedagogical ideas working in tandem, the lives and writing of our children will be in the foreground and the books written by the adults will just be reference material for their schoolwork, and we will feel that adapting our teaching method to their needs will be maximized.

> Other educators must have had this dream,[1] but we were able to see it come to fruition. Printing in the classroom is now available to all the schools – even the poor ones. We are certain that through our teaching, many more schools will join our group.[2]

Freinet was also thinking about the printer Jacques Collombat (1668-1744), who tutored the future King Louis XV in 1718 and printed some of the young king's work. Though Freinet greatly admired Paul Robin, who had great success with printing at the Cempuis orphanage, and Ovide Decroly's extensive usage of the printing press in his Ermitage school in Brussels,[3] he wanted his students to run their own presses and dirty their fingers with black ink . . .today, we would call this interactive. He wanted his students to take pride in their own work: from concept to mailing it out and the multitude of the in-between steps.

Freinet and his Students' Writing

On January 1, 1920, the ministry of education assigned Freinet to teach at the elementary boys' school of Bar-sur-Loup,[4] which consisted of two classrooms. As a novice teacher, when he entered these classrooms, he saw a relic from the nineteenth century: desks with their own benches aligned in rows, a high teacher's platform, coat hangers affixed on the wall, unclean sanitary facilities, and a broken-down blackboard. In the 1952 movie *L'École Buissonnière*, one of the early scenes depicts quite accurately what "le nouveau maître"(played by Bernard Blier, as M. Pascal) saw when he entered his old and decrepit school.

Although Maria Montessori already vigorously denounced the poor working conditions of teachers in Italy and the outdated tools used by their students, Freinet was soon going to lend his powerful voice to obtain concrete changes for the teachers and the students.

For Freinet, it was his first discovery of students. In his notebook which replaced the one he kept during WWI and his convalescence, he noted the day-to-day remarks of his students, their observations and movements as they hurried to accomplish their tasks. To him, this traditional teaching method, which requires an excessive concentration at an aberrant rhythm, was a major reason why students failed. Or why did this method fail its students. Freinet often asked himself: Why do these lessons never start with motivating the students? Why do we have this *culture* to transmit?

One day, he noticed that Joseph, his happy-go-lucky student—the one who was always barefoot, dressed with the same shirt and whose pants were held up with a rope—forgot to go into the classroom because a blue caterpillar slowly crawling on the wall across the school fascinated him. On another day, always carrying small critters in his pockets or in a special box, he organized a snail race on his desk that enthralled all the students. Freinet was mindful of the passion his students exhibited while watching the snail race, and encouraging the grey-green, the chestnut, or even the grey-black snail to win:

> That's it! Is it the grey-green? Yes, it's the grey-green snail that's winning! The whole classroom was vibrant, and full of life, hands were extending and ready to grab the three snails. Quickly, Joseph snared his menagerie and put them back in his matchbox.[5]

As soon as race ended, the teacher was already writing on the blackboard:

> *Allons les enfants!* Let's write on the blackboard what happened with this snail race.[6]

After writing the description of the race on the blackboard, Freinet realized that, once erased, there would be no record of this exciting event in his students' lives. Feeling guilty for having to erase the text written on the blackboard, he thought:

- What if the students print their own texts?
- Was printing a text the only solution for maintaining a permanent record of their effort?
- Would a printed page add another dimension to this event?
- Would it be a good source for writing, reading, and discoveries?

Although the snail race was only the catalyst, ideas about printing in the classroom were already germinating in Freinet's mind. Since his adolescence, he was an avid reader, and during his long and difficult recovery from the war wounds, he became more introverted and read many more books. Now, he had the luxury of time and didn't have to report to a new teaching post until he felt well enough. While convalescing in the hospital, he read about education, the philosophy of education and a multitude of teaching methods.

He traveled to Grasse[7] to talk to printers, who advised him against launching such an adventure and sneered at him, *"Your students will hoard all the letters; they will even steal them,"* but he disregarded their negative comments. Freinet purchased a type of rudimentary press, the CINUP, from an advertisement and received it a few days later.

It was like a magic tool that everybody discovered together: Letters, composing sticks, and the first printed sheet. To purchase this equipment, he mortgaged his future paychecks. Due to a lack of paper, he recycled old voting bulletins and old notebooks used by a Bavarian cooperative.

Through perseverance (regular assembly of letters, inking and bookbinding), the results became markedly better.

The 1952 movie *L'École Buissonnière* faithfully captured the new teacher (Monsieur Pascal) bringing the printer and the letters to his students. One of them became so excited that he understood what Gutenberg said after he saw the very first page he printed: *"Et la lumière fut!"*[8]

A few months later he purchased another press with a stock of paper in Grasse, which he paid from his own savings and by not going on vacation. After experimenting with it every day, he described in *Clarté*[9] a first theoretical approach to his work:

> A good teacher could organize a succession of lessons and homework that would fit the needs and the interests of the class. But, what on which printed schoolbook could the student practice his reading, which needs non-stop effort?

> Although the teacher could look at school manuals arranged by "center of interests," those based on Ovide Decroly's ideas are a marked improvement over those produced by the Ministry of Education, but it is still not enough to keep the interest up, because reading – like life – is not static and evolves constantly.

> This renewed technique [of printing] is all about discovery and a fact hit me. When I browse the set of titles of the 200 pages of our *Books of Life* [compilation of texts printed by the students in the first two quarters], I note that the distribution of topics is essentially the one that partisans of "centers of interest" recommend.

> Here is the fall season with its fruits, mushrooms, and high winds. There is winter with the various means to guarantee us the cold weather. The spring, so rich with impressions, with strong rains, hail, rocks falling, the first flowers and battles of flowers, the richly decorated visiting circuses and the colds and flu that usually empty our classes.

> Contrary to the method recommended by Decroly, I note with satisfaction and humility that these Books of Life are replete with topics that interest my students. There are no imposed topics as I am satisfied to listen, direct the conversation, synthesize and put in order their ideas.

Freinet concluded, *"Leave the textbook, and let our students live."*

The Printing Press in the Classroom

Freinet acted as a central point for distributing the necessary material for printing the school journals. He provided characters for printing in their proper spacing and various inks that were the same as those used in the typographic trade. He always chose material useful to his friends and disciples.

He spent many long hours perfecting printing. In 1924, with his first CINUP printing press, Freinet was able to print only four or five lines at a time. Over the years, it evolved from a roller press, to a wooden press, to another different type of automatic press—until he perfected it into a very simple aluminum-built press meant to simplify the fulfillment of his vision.

At the time the printing press was first introduced to disadvantaged schools, it was set up in a very rudimentary fashion. It consisted of a press, the composing stick and the lettering which were placed on a small table (or a trestle), and four or five students congregated around it. Over the years, this setup improved when he was able to expand the printing room with better presses and more space for his students to work on creating texts.

Freinet could not have envisioned that his ideas would evolve into what we have today. Our "printing presses" are so complex yet so easy to use that even a first-grader can use a laser printer and produce, in a few minutes, what Freinet's students labored over for many hours . . . and their hands did not get blackened by ink!

Less than two years after Freinet introduced the notion of printing in his classroom, Eugène Villermoz (1878-1960), a columnist for the Parisian newspaper *Le Temps*, praised Freinet in the July 4, 1926 article called, "A L'École de Gutenberg." In this article, Villermoz noted the most salient points about Freinet and his new teaching method:

> This teacher bought a hand press that does not represent a considerable expense. His other expenses were purchasing ink, paper and the yearly melting and recasting of the lead-based letters. He invited his students to narrate and write what interests them. Afterwards, they coordinated better narrations and prepared these texts for printing, the chosen pages are read aloud in the classroom. They all listen with rapt attention to this reading.[10]

This was a very astute observation, and Freinet quickly realized that the word"printing" conferred dignity and prestige that the children deeply felt. To see their thoughts transferred into metal, it assures them a flattering appearance of solidity and everlastingness. Every mobile character is a small pedestal that supports the statue of a letter. On the composing stick, one prepares the glorification of a word and the apotheosis of a sentence.

To Villermoz and Freinet, working on printing constitutes an operation of the intelligence very different from the one that consists of "blackening a school notebook." In the printing process, one chooses his words with infinitely more care and respect when one wonders if they are going to receive the honors of the composition, to clothe the uniform of regiments of Gutenberg and to parade in an impeccable order under the attentive and amazed eyes of the reading crowd.

Besides being pedagogically sound, this is an excellent method. To form the words by juxtaposing metallic letters, it is to fix them mechanically in his visual memory, to photograph them and to possess them more intensely than sketching its silhouette with the tip of a feather or a pencil. Villermoz concluded by saying that:

> Printing gives a personal and independent life to words. It is an excellent test, not only for spelling, but also for the grammar, the syntax, the logical analysis and the color of style. There exists a 'metallic' style as there previously existed an 'epistolary' style.[11]

Freinet used all these secret movements of our instinct very ingeniously. He obtained excellent results and collected excellent *Books of Their Lives* every year from the hands of his young printers. Extending his action, he exchanged this book with teachers with similar work, executed in the same conditions by schoolchildren from schools in the Rhône Valley.[12] Not only did Villermoz validate Freinet's work outside his small village, he also validated him outside his work in education.

Lettering and Inking

At the onset of his innovative pedagogical experiment, Freinet purchased a great variety of tiles: letters in lower- and uppercase format, punctuation, Roman and Arab numerals as well as blank tiles for spacing. These characters were in semi-soft metal (lead was the main ingredient) and were made to last several years.

Following their first usage, the students melted down, recast, and re-used the characters. They were numerous enough to allow five or six-team of students to work together by placing these characters in composing sticks.

He also purchased inks in different colors and viscosities as well as papers in different colors, rollers and brushes. "Student-inkers" got their hands all blackened while inking the texts, but it was a task they all wanted to do because it was useful and entertaining. Freinet used to say, "If the ink has blackened your hands, just wash them."

Illustrating the Texts

It was a very slow evolution. In Freinet's first printed material, he had either no illustrations or only duplicates of drawings. He studied, experimented with, used and perfected multiple means to prepare typographic plates: labels on wood, copper, tin plates, cardboard and especially engraving on linoleum with special tools. With these techniques, he maximized the use of artistic illustrations for educational purposes.

To develop this technique, Freinet and his students endured a very slow-going collaborative process. He was quick to point out, when his students illustrated the first journal in Bar-sur-Loup (*La Gerbe*), that he was only a collaborator and the discovery of the joys of illustrating the texts rested mainly with the students.

The first texts printed by the students were just plain texts with sketchy, clumsy illustrations. They experimented with various techniques to enhance their texts with illustrations, e.g., using sketches made of zinc, wood (not recommended because hardwood was very expensive), copper and cardboard (developed by a teacher from another school and easy to use by kindergarten students).

Finally, the students settled on engraving on linoleum as the most economical, and the best possible medium to produce excellent artistic and pedagogical material to incorporate in the printing of the texts.

Preparing to Print

From 1924 to 1930, Freinet experimented on how to best utilize this pedagogical tool that attracted so many educators in France and the rest of Europe. He simultaneously developed the following complementary aspects to the printing press:

- Livres de Vie (books of life)
- Le Texte Libre (free text)
- Le Journal Scolaire (school journal)
- Les Échanges Interscolaires (Interscholastic Exchanges)
- La Correspondance Interscolaire (interscholastic correspondence)
- Les Échanges d'Enfants (students' exchanges)

This chapter covers the first three topics of this list—the other three will be covered in a subsequent chapter—and their use for developing students' critical skills: Reading, writing, grammar, arithmetic and critical thinking.

The Books of Life

At the beginning of the school year, each student was provided with two empty binders. In one, he filed his daily work (homework, material he printed or letters he wrote, etc.), and it became the *Book of My Life*. In the other, he filed everything he received from his distant correspondents, whether printed material or letters, and that became the *Book of Their Lives*.

For Freinet, giving students blank binders was based on very sound pedagogical tenets akin to John Locke's *tabula rasa*, since the students come to school with a blank mind, are given a blank binder and fill it with whatever acquired knowledge they are able to master in and out of class. In this type of classroom, students are in control of their destinies guided by the teacher's gentle hand and wise advice. Freinet gave another voice to his students by letting them choose what they wanted to study, write about, and print.

Traditionally, teachers gave students a fact-filled textbook of topics they knew nothing about and had to cram because the teacher was told by official decrees when, where and what to study. When Freinet discarded the textbooks from the Ministry of Education, he was prepared to fight with the Establishment, as they were in control of his destiny.

In July 1926, Freinet and his students produced a small twelve-page booklet[13] of a lovely child's story, bound and illustrated. The class produced 200 copies. Freinet took his students' "labor of love" to a teachers' convention in Tours,[14] where he hoped he would receive accolades and acceptance of his highly innovative approach. On the contrary, all he received was scorn and criticism:

> Unfortunately, nobody seemed interested in our effort. They felt it was a crazy idea. What interest do you think the children will have in reading these simple texts, so near to their own lives . . . Give them Hugo, La Fontaine or Sand! That's literature.[15]

In the 1950s, the PCF unleashed its wrath and attacked Freinet because he gave more credence to what his students wrote than to the "great books of literature," written by authors like Victor Hugo or Voltaire. In fact, Freinet was simultaneously attacked by the Right for not following their orders (educational decrees), and by the Left for not following their orders (communist pedagogical theories).

Freinet developed his teaching techniques by using strong foundations tailor-made to the needs of his students. The Freinet classes were born, and the practice of these exercises validated their existence. Many teachers followed this technique and became ardent adherents to Freinet's ideas, and even a few school inspectors begrudgingly admitted that it was a viable teaching method.

In many departmental *écoles normales* (schools of education) the Freinet Technique were taught to future educators, and in nearly all departments, classes had printing machines in working condition, and the teachers were applying these techniques. Slowly but surely, many of Freinet's ideas started influencing the traditional pedagogy, and many more educators embraced his technique. Despite the attacks on his teaching methods, Freinet—like Don Quixote tilting windmills—moved blithely along knowing that he was doing the right thing for his poor proletarian students.

The Free Text

In the beginning of the twentieth century, the traditional teaching method in France was that all the students needed, other than the teacher's knowledge, were the official text books to be utilized according to strict official decrees. To implement this, the academic world devised an abundance of methods, processes and even deceitful tricks to validate what they called "the scholastic" approach to teaching. Freinet tried to change this attitude when he introduced the idea of the free text[16].

Free texts were not random writing exercises on any subject. They were meaningful texts his students wrote when they had something to say. hey wrote when they wanted and on any topic that pleased them. Freinet found that the students always wrote meaningfully when an event or an emotion strongly affected them. Freinet also said:

> Many of the students will write their spontaneous texts sitting on the side of the big dining table, on a notebook placed on their knees listening to their grandmother tell stories about the past, or on the school bag, before entering the classroom. Most assuredly, now they write during the hours assigned for their free time.[17]

The free text was also a reflection of life, their lives. The student had a clear concept, and he expressed it in his own language. It might have been clumsy, and grammatically imperfect, but it was always natural and moving. This is what one student's observation of a hail storm:

> Hail storms started in March at three o'clock. Many hail stones as big as marbles came down and made noises like drum rolls on roof tiles and windows. In a few minutes, the countryside was all white. We were very

happy to be home, the mothers were making balls of wool, and the fathers were bemoaning the fate of their countryside.[18]

And furthermore Freinet observed that:

> Each of my students wrote about it. After they wrote about it, they had very enthusiastic discussions on hail storms. Then a few students sat in front of the printing press. It took them 15-20 minutes to compose a lively text, and they even checked their spelling and grammar, they did not need me. Meanwhile, the other students continued their assigned tasks: individual reading, copying or homework related to the day's teaching, or arithmetic homework based on self-teaching methods.[19]

Why did the students write these texts even though they hated traditional dictations? They wrote because these texts will be printed in their school journal, and will be read by other students, parents and schools inside and outside of France. Freinet found that being flexible, having a variety of centers of learning and interests enlivened classroom discussions and generated more successful topics for printing. He declared:

> The natural tendency for the students and their teachers, who have just started with free texts in their classroom, is to narrate events in their daily lives: The village, the neighborhood, their vacation or at a Sunday picnic. Here we have a chance to find the child in his most natural habitat, to see his own life, to explore his innermost topics of interest and the vibrancy of the world around him. We do not need to resort to outside influences or give him textbooks alien to his life. The students find in the school a direct link between their life and what they are learning.
>
> For example, we can discuss and write about the following topics: the missing book, the chicken, the raft, falling from the bicycle, the cow in the well, the circus in town, hunting, and the migrant bird. These texts and discussions are at the basis of a successful pedagogical approach.[20]

The advantages to this technique came from the fact that most students want to just compose, print their text, and not be forced to learn in the more traditional scholastic[21] approach: The traditional grammar, arithmetic, geography or science books. Freinet viewed this method as a *dead scholastic* since it might inhibit their activities and totally snuff out the vitality they exhibited in their classroom efforts. Thirty years after its introduction, the free text became an accepted teaching tool, and Freinet was then able to say:[22]

Let's not fool ourselves. Acceptance of free text, even in official circles, did not fall from the sky like manna from heaven. It was a slow and stubborn process to conquer many stubborn educators, who wound up loving our method. Now we can say with conviction that using free texts in the classroom:
   • Fascinates the children, writers and readers alike, because one day the readers can become writers
   • Opens their minds, effectively and pedagogically speaking, to learning the basic elements of culture
   • Allows us to introduce our highly recommended pedagogical tenets
   • Changes the atmosphere in the classroom because it changes the dynamic between teachers and students. In our schools, the teachers consider the students as flowers that are about to bloom, and we have to nurse them to from bud to full bloom.[23]

When Freinet introduced this concept of the free text in his classrooms, he believed it was part of the bigger concept he called *the pedagogical exploitation of the free text*, and it was only a step in integrating the various pedagogical aspects that derived from that October day in 1924 when he introduced printing in his Bar-sur-Loup classroom.

The School Journal

It is interesting to note the evolution of the vocabulary employed in Freinet's pamphlet. It seems that "the school journal" began to counterbalance "printing." It also seems that after having discovered printing in 1924 and focusing all his energies on the "printed sheet," the idea of turning it into a "school journal"—which was born later—became the logical extension of the system that Freinet was putting *in situ*.

Printing was the magic tool that allowed the students to attain a more significant stature: Freinet assembled the printed sheets that circulated in the village in order to present them to his colleagues. The idea to combine the best pages was the seed of the first characteristics of a newspaper. One of his students said:[24]

A school journal is a cohesive project. It makes no sense to compile all kinds of articles and to bind them together. What we need is a sense of unity and a structure. The school journal must be generated by our actions and produce reactions.

When Freinet began the Interscholastic Exchanges, these journals were printed on a regular basis. For Freinet, the school journal was not going to replace printing, it was a parallel effort, part of the same logical chain created to teach the students.

How to Produce a School Journal

The most basic step in producing a school journal was the judicious use of the manuscript. To reach that point, the collaborative texts were written by students and their teachers, and elaborated upon on the blackboard. Once this step was completed, the students transferred the information into their notebooks.

If carbon paper was available, they inserted one or two to produce more than one copy to keep a record. One would stay in the student's *Book of Life*, but the other one was integrated into the *Book of Their Lives*. The school journal would be the logical extension of the existing written texts. In a class of twenty students, it was reasonable to assume that after a few days of work, there would be enough material for a school journal.

Copying the texts from the blackboard onto a sheet of paper was not a chore. It became a collective body of work in which each student imparted something special, whether it was a story about his family, a drawing of his farm or anything he felt "the world should know about." At the end of the month, the students' product was bound, and everyone in the village got a chance to read it before it was sent out to their correspondents. At his suggestion, Freinet noted that soldiers and prisoners also followed this practice of making note of events on paper in the Chibron concentration camp where he was jailed in 1941. He toyed with other printing methods (stenciling was one), but his best success was the printing press.

For Freinet, the school journal could only exist as a corollary to a printed text because the printed text was far superior to any other method of reproduction, especially superior to a stenciled text, which is hard to read since the impression fades very quickly. Students were enamored with seeing their texts printed because the illustrations improved their words.

Although composing a text for printing was a slow and fastidious process, it allowed the students to bond with their compositions and to see their words and texts come alive. The students gave life to their own words, but also made sure the grammar and facts were correct. This was the role of the students: to police themselves, discuss the content and be gently prodded by the teacher's benevolent presence.

At these times, Freinet was their friend and partner, not the overwhelming know-it-all individual perched on a rostrum looking down on his students. The students who embarked on this journey of discovery, where "a simple word starts with a single letter," were heroes to themselves because they mastered the word and made it work to their advantage.

An Interview With Freinet

Two days after the July 4, 1926 article in *Le Temps* was published—and since Bar-sur-Loup was so close to Nice—G. Davin De Champlos, a reporter from *L'Éclaireur de Nice et du Sud-Ouest*, went there to interview Freinet and to ask him the details of this new teaching method.[25]

In this picturesque, quaint and archaic town, the 100-year-old elms and the old fountain that sang the same cool songs for centuries coexisted with the school housed on the ground floor of the town hall. The school was old, like everything that surrounded it: its walls flaked lamentably, the benches and the tables showed their wear and tear from many generations of students applying their elbows or digging in with their thick-soled shoes. As he was reaching his destination, this is what he saw:

> Twenty-five youngsters, five are ten-years old, have just returned from the midday break and are jostling on the way to taking their seats. A young man barely 30 years old – with brown and romantic hair, pulled back as if to let us discover a forehead bubbling with ideas, tries to put some order in this chaos: it is Monsieur Freinet.

Freinet seemed quite pleased that *L'Éclaireur de Nice* came to 'unearth' him in his eagles' aerie, and told the journalist that he did not do anything so extraordinary . . . he merely had a simple idea and applied it as best as he could.

> Freinet told me[26] that Bar-sur-Loup was his first assignment and that the Academic Inspector named him to it six years ago, in 1918. He was going to graduate from a teachers' training school in Nice (École Normale de Nice) when WWI started and he left for the war in 1915 like everyone else. Upon his return, the position at Bar-sur-Loup was waiting for him.

Freinet explained to the journalist how he transformed his twenty-five students into student-printers:

> I am happy to take my students on walks. We observe people and things that we meet on the road; then, once we are back in school, we crystallize these observations into writing. Once we write it on the blackboard, it teaches the

students handwriting. It does not leave a really strong impression on their brains because it quickly gets erased. This was when I decided to let them print what they wrote on the blackboard.

From the very beginning, I was struck by the results I obtained. Not only did the students learn all their letters very quickly, but they also learned them while composing what they read in literature books, books vastly different from those on which the students just applied their intelligence.

When the journalist asked Freinet if the youngest students were quick on picking up the composing techniques for printing, he replied:

Incroyable! It's quite unbelievable! The youngest ones, the five-year-olds, have adapted to it with as much ease as the older ones. In a very short time, they managed with an astonishing facility. Do not imagine that their work on the printing press disgusts them or diverts them from their regular learning. To the contrary, they ask me to let them learn math and history.

A major difficulty emerged at the beginning of Freinet's experiment. He had to find a printing press that was convenient, easy to use and relatively inexpensive. He solved that problem when he discovered the CINUP, an extremely simple hand press with many characters and very similar to the one professional typographers had used before the invention of linotype:

Once this press was purchased other expenses are very low: paper and ink throughout the year, and melting down the worn-out characters ... and that is all. We printed, this year, about 550 pages of eight lines, and our material always held up.

It allows us to communicate with other schools. Thus, since last October, we have corresponded with a class of the school of boys in Villeurbanne. We are dedicated to a very active exchange of printed material and Books of Life. In his own binder every child accumulates his daily typographic tests. It ends up constituting the more attractive and most instructive of the reading books.

Three other schools have just bought material for printing, and we are going to get in touch with them. You would not know to believe this movement of exchanging pages, printed material, postcards, maps and letters constitutes an intellectual profit and state of mind for our school children.

Finally, the journalist asked Freinet if his initiative was really an innovation. This is what Freinet said:

Yes, because of how I shaped it. At Doctor Decroly's Ermitage school in Brussels, it was the teachers who printed their real newspaper, The School Courier. In Rome, Maria Montessori gave her students rough blocks of wood with which they would be able to draw letters, then words, then sentences. Their methods have no relationship with my method that consists of sitting a five- to six- year-old who hardly knows fifteen to twenty letters of the alphabet, at the composition table, putting a composing stick in his hands, and letting him compose.

Freinet pointed to another advantage of this system:

A well-known text and seeing the student print it. Not only is this technique new but, I think it is one that is complete and passionate.

As Freinet's students began to act impatient with the questioning, the classroom was starting to rumble, and the journalist took leave of this man of initiative and audacity to whom *Le Temps* dedicated a justified laudatory chronicle. *L'Éclaireur de Nice* also owed it to Freinet to let people know that this native son of the Maritime-Alps had a beautiful idea and had courageously brought it to fruition.

What Were These Rules of Perfection?

Though the students created the school journal that formed the original presentation, Freinet insisted that they adhere to and follow five strict rules to attain maximum perfection:[27]

1. The school journal must be a well-printed document
Its perfection is a sine qua non condition for its success. For this, not only must the text be grammatically correct, but also the group of students assigned to it must work as a cohesive team, which includes the inking and clarity of the printing.
2. The text must be 'justified'
This simply means that the width of the text to print should be in proportion to its length.
3. The pagination is very important
According to Freinet, the art of printing is based on the art of pagination. A text must have an airy and breezy look about it . . . not compacted letters and lines. It is akin to the canvas of an artist whose finished product should make him proud of his masterpiece, and this is what Freinet wanted and expected from his students to produce.

4. The text must be perfect and without any typographical mistake

The students must have pride in their work and not let typographical errors ruin the text. Conversely, the teacher must give his final approval before the printing.

5. The students must illustrate the school journal

The illustrations should reflect the students' interests in their own lives and environment. Freinet believed that if the school journal was 'pleasant to look at,' if the content was the students' original expression, and if it reflected their lives and interests, then it would interest parents and correspondents.

The students (and their teachers) followed his rules, and the school journal was a successful pedagogical idea.

Psychological Advantages of the School Journal

Freinet felt that the success or the failure of his pedagogical method hinged on the psychological advantages it offered, and he knew that he met the conditions for success. Here is an analysis of some of the psychological factors behind his success in implementing a school journal.

When the student writes or prints his free text, psychology does not enter the equation. More likely, he does not even question if the work he produces will help readers understand him better. But to a teacher, the work produced by this student will show a marked improvement in the following five areas.

1. Normalizing the Student's Environment

In the past, the world of the classroom was perceived as being different from the student's home and social life—and society has always thrived on maintaining this duality. Freinet thought that this "split personality" has always been harmful since most students were unable to go back and forth from one world to another. In his classrooms, the students came to school from home and all their familial preoccupations, and they did not have to switch from one life into another. School, home, village and friends were all part of their normal school day.

2. A New Discipline – Discipline through Enjoyable Work

Rather than the teachers disciplining the students, they fall into a mode of self-discipline based on the motivation that "the work must get done." It meant the total production of the school journal: From writing the manuscript to mailing the finished product to their correspondents.

It seems that the pride in having done a good job, and on time, was their only motives.

3. Free Expression of the Children

For too many years, neither the schools nor the official ministerial decrees legislated that children could emote their feelings in the classroom. They legislated only what had to be taught in the classroom and how the teacher should impart it to his students. No allowances were ever made to give the students a voice, a voice to sing, to yell, or to express their innermost feelings, as they were all suppressed. Through the free text and school journal, the students were given many avenues to express their feelings. Their spontaneity was definitely an asset when it would be time for them to learn, study or print their texts since these actions were not considered chores, but normal extensions of their daily lives.

4. Fruitful Work

An anonymous British author once said: "Useless work drives crazy those who have to do it." Whoever this author was, and Freinet was very adept at not naming the sources of many of his ideas and quotations,[28] he definitely believed that schools were like factories that did not offer happiness "on the job," where the workers "slaved away" and did not "revere the notion of work." Although Freinet knew that he was going overboard in painting such a bleak picture, the fact remains that many schools "make work" for students: Cram, pass the exams, and earn a living with a decent job. With the school journal as the prototype for learning, students do not need to know or do extra work – it's all there. Students are dedicated because their happiness is learning through hard and enjoyable work.

5. A Pedagogy of Success

In Freinet's own words:

> Produce a beautiful school journal. Be technically well prepared so that without taking any undue risks your success will be recognized. Little by little, you will be able to accentuate – in your classroom and in your life – the success that gives hope, drive and energy. You will slowly discard the paraphernalia associated with failure (homework, punishment, exams) that reinforce failure.[29]

Freinet strongly believed that "practice makes perfect," and he maintained this attitude throughout his lifetime. He had his share of success, failures, victories and defeats but always maintained his equanimity through it all.

Pedagogical Advantages of the School Journal

Freinet saw four pedagogical advantages when the free text/school journal became the mainstay in the classroom.

1. The School Journal Allows the Teacher to Better Impart his Knowledge

At the various teaching levels, kindergarten, elementary or middle school, the teacher will be able to communicate better with his students because he will not be bound by traditional dictation methods or harp on about grammar. The students will bring their natural curiosity to the classroom, and therefore the teacher will have a classroom brimming with activity and not bound by the traditional teaching and learning methods.

2. The School Journal is Like a Permanent Window on the World

Freinet thought that a school, which uses the school journal at the major center for teaching, could not be considered any more as outmoded. Instead, it is a school on the verge of being a modern school.

3. The School Journals Are the Live Archives of the Classroom

A problem with the traditional schools is that they do not leave a meaningful trace of the classroom's existence. What was on the blackboard was quickly erased, and the students' notes were quickly thrown out at the end of each school year. With printing in the classroom and the school journal, students, teachers, and parents near or far, will have mementos of events in their children lives. Freinet said to his fellow teachers:

> Write a school journal. You and your students will be proud of your common masterpiece. You will only feel pride that you brought to your classroom the certainty that you are on the right track of progress. These archives will bring only bring memories to the writers and correspondents.[30]

These archives will come alive and will relate and narrate events from the points of view of those who lived it.

4. You Will Have a Masterpiece to Show

When the farmer shows off his prize cow, when the homemaker gives you a taste of her prized baked apple pie, and when the artist displays his latest painting on his easel, they all display their pride. Although the teacher does not have a thing in his classroom to highlight his hard work and his devotion, he knows—and so do the parents—that a beautifully calligraphied page is neither a student's masterpiece, nor a well-written table of multiplication, but it is an original "artwork."

On the other hand, writing into the Book of Life or printing a text for the school journal falls into the category of "daily masterpieces." It is a bridge between mastering a manual activity, a creative and thinking skill, and feeding the students' souls because it pushes them to go beyond the limits of who they are supposed to be and what they are supposed to do. The school journal is a major production, which touches on all facets of the students' education, and in which they all participated.

The teacher's role was to ensure that his students liked what they do and, like an actor who enjoys his trade, were paid for doing something they enjoy. These were the major pedagogical and psychological advantages of having a school journal as the basis for teaching.

This worked quite well in 1924 and, throughout Freinet's lifetime, even when his relationship with the French government, various ministers of education, the mayors of the towns in which he lived, the school inspectors, the parents and, even, the French communist party, were uneasy and strained.[31]

How Did Freinet Set Up his Teaching Method?

Freinet never intended to change the teaching method abruptly and brusquely since he knew that it would work only after a long period of trial and error. He never wanted to remove the textbooks mandated by the Ministry of Education until he was ready to substitute them with a foolproof method.

To start with, Freinet insisted that printing in the classroom would not be a boring endeavor. By allowing the students to create their Books of Life, the teachers would realize that this lively method of teaching was far superior to the official textbooks he believed were useless and soon to be abandoned. In fact, he advised his followers not to discard the existing method before building a new one.

What he did was follow, in his own way, some of the Minister of Education's decrees. This is what he declared:

> These ministerial instructions must be more than an encouragement, they must be like our prayer book. They agree, almost totally with our teaching method and our 15-year long battle and perseverance to implement changes. Maybe the future will show that we were right. It is a tough role always to be at the forefront of progress.

Freinet's attitude was interesting because he always used the ambiguities built into the ministerial decrees to justify his actions. Freinet developed this art form quite early in his life. It was in his genes, as a native of a village of the High-Alps, to mock the authorities with a smile. He did it many times and got away with it even more times!

Conclusion: Legalizing the School Journal

Approximately twenty-five years after its "creation," the school journal became a hot topic at the French National Assembly. Between the years 1951 and 1953, the legal status of the school journal became very important in light of the debate of whether to grant it the special mailing privileges other journals and newspapers enjoyed.

The deputies took up the debates on the validity of the school journal as a key pedagogical method, and at the National Assembly, Deputy Jean-Marie Flandrin asked the Prime Minister to grant the school journals this privilege:

> In 1951, more than 5,000 schools produced a school journal. Academic inspectors, teachers, parents, and students are deeply interested in this method. It's been a long time—more than twenty-five years now—that these school journals have been circulating as periodicals and are fulfilling all the necessary conditions to be granted these special rates . . . but it looks now that some newspapers opposed to this method are opposed to us giving them the special postal rate they richly deserve.

> This is not the first time that such a roadblock was erected. The former Prime Minister was asked on April 20, 1951, to intervene with the minister in charge of the Postal Service to give the school newspapers the special mailing rate. This minister invoked Article 90 of the Finance Law of April 16, 1930, stating that 'special newspaper rates are only granted to general interest publications geared to educate and inform the public at large,' denying their request.

> Sir, under what purely arbitrary whim did the minister decide to aver that school journals do not fulfill the conditions of that 1930 law? Many authorizations were given to periodicals that do not serve education or promote our national unity. Some of these even promoted hate and dissension. Mr. Minister, I ask you to please intervene so that school journals are quickly granted such privileges. By easing the circulation of the school journals, you will become a defender of the logic behind its use and you will be helping to develop an excellent element at the forefront of modern pedagogy.[32]

The amendment to the April 16, 1930, law was unanimously passed, and the school journals were finally accepted as full-fledged newspapers useful in the classroom. Freinet was vindicated and proven correct.

From the time Freinet died in 1966 to today, the technology evolved tremendously. Yet, the fact remains that the teacher's active role is minimal, and this pedagogy relegates his role to merely posing questions, gently probing and guiding the students. *They interact with him, and he is the moderator.* This is the basis of critical thinking, and it still goes on in the schools of France to this day.

NOTES

1. He was referring to Pestalozzi, Robin, Decroly and Sanderson.
2. Freinet, Célestin. "Matériel d'imprimerie." *L'Imprimerie à l'École.* Bulletin No. 6. pp. 1-4. Juin 1927.
3. In the Ermitage and Cempuis schools, the teachers printed from texts supplied by their students.
4. Located in the Maritime-Alps department, close to Cannes.
5. In: Élise Freinet, *Naissance d'une pédagogie populaire*, p. 32.
6. Ibid. p. 32.
7. A small town in the South of France, 20 miles north of Nice.
8. And the light went up!
9. Freinet, . "L'imprimerie à l'École." *Clarté.* No. 75. pp. 259-61. Juin 1925.
10. Villermoz, Eugène. "A L'École de Gutenberg." *Le Temps.* p.1. Paris. 4 juillet 1926.
11. Ibid.
12. Villermoz mentioned a school in Lyon (M. Primas?), but Daniel was Freinet's first correspondent.
13. Enfantines: Histoire d'un petit garçon dans la montagne (*Story of a young boy in the mountain*). Juillet 1926.
14. Tours: city located approximately 160 miles southwest of Paris.
15. Freinet, Célestin. "Le texte libre." *Bibliothèque de l'École Moderne.* No. 3. p. 7. Cannes. 1960.
16. Freinet, Célestin. "Les Techniques Freinet." *BENP.* No. 80. Mars 1953.
17. Freinet, Célestin." Le texte libre." *BEM.* No. 3. p. 13. Cannes. 1960.
18. Anonymous.
19. Ibid. p. 10.
20. Ibid. p. 62.
21. The term "scholastic" derives from a Christian philosophical movement. Today, it simply refers to a pedagogical approach that's far from a social reality and the needs of the pupils.
22. Ibid. p. 9-10.
23. *BEM,* no. 3, p. 9-10.
24. Anonymous quote.
25. De Champlos, G. Davin. L'Éducation par la Typographie. *L'Éclaireur de Nice et du Sud-Ouest.* Nice. 6 juillet 1926.
26. "Me" refers to G. Davin de Champlos, the reporter.

27. Freinet, Célestin. *Le Journal Scolaire*. Éditions Rossignol, Montmorillon. 1957. pp. 35-38.

28. As explained in Acker's *Célestin Freinet*. Greenwood Press. July 2000.

29. Freinet, C. *Le Journal Scolaire*. pp. 84-85. Éd. Rossignol, Montmorillon. 1957.

30. Ibid. p. 68.

31. For more information on these struggles, see *Célestin Freinet* by V. Acker.

32. Minutes of the Third Plenary session of the National Assembly. December 19, 1951.

Chapter 4
Implementing the Freinet Method Today

Among the many educational methods "invented" years ago, the Freinet Method is still alive in France and in many other countries around the world, but not in the United States or other English-speaking countries. This document condenses the many interpretations of how the Freinet-based schools in France implement his technique. The charter that the Freinet schools adhere to addresses these issues:

1. Educational principles and policies
2. Internal regulation
3. The cooperative management of the Freinet teams
4. How the teams are formed in the various Freinet schools
5. Assessing the Freinet teams
6. The training and formation between teams
7. Developing relationships with partners, parents, etc.
8. Contacts ruling the cooperation of the Freinet teams.

Preamble

Since the Freinet teams advocate the continuity of education from kindergarten to university, they refer to themselves as teachers, and the generic term school is in continuous use.

1. Educational Principles and Policies
A society that is built on liberty, equality and fraternity needs responsible, autonomous people, capable of critiquing the world in which they live in order to finalize the modus operandi of the Charter of the Modern School (Freinet school). The Freinet teams function within the context of non-denominational schools (lay schools) and serve within the parameters of the Minister of Education, since they obtain the same

financial benefits and conditions as other schools. With this in place, the teams can easily interchange ideas and goals since the diffusion and portability of their practices and workings create a successful environment in which the children can blossom.

Because particular attention must be given to the public schools whose systems are culturally distant, there is the need to be socially heterogeneous to create a success story. Since the Freinet teams are located in more manageable and smaller-sized schools, they champion small-school structures able to evolve within large public schools. Within this context, the teachers in these child-centered schools must:

- Recognize the child as a person
- Respect the children's rhythm of work and accept their cultural and social heritages, as well as their personalities
- Accept what life bestows on the children
- Give every child the recognition he needs to grow and develop
- Encourage the development of an autonomous sense of critical thinking that will allow each participant to take full responsibility
- Encourage freedom of expression within a team
- Be capable of training and teaching the acquisition of knowledge based on the methods introduced by Freinet
- Offer access, regardless of hierarchy and field of education, to different techniques of knowledge in a global, polytechnic education.

Additionally, this educational project should be successful because it's based on Freinet's pedagogical tenets that are already implemented by cooperative teams of teachers within *écoles primaires* (elementary schools), *collèges* (junior high schools) and *lycées* (public high schools).

Freinet's pedagogy encompasses educational research relating to education and the International Convention of Children's Rights, which recognizes the rights of the children and their special status to:

- Train to become top students
- Jointly be responsible for the life of their team and school.

The status of the teachers within this structure is to be:

- Responsible for their schools' implementation of agreed-upon projects that their students undertake
- Meet on a regular basis

• Widen the team by recruiting others (children and adults) who share the school life
• Responsible for the consistency of the final work produced and the security of children
• Part of a cooperative effort, each person's role being defined by what he brings to the team. The aim remains to hold the child responsible for his role in the total concept of globalization.

This educational continuum will last for as long as the child is in the care of a teacher it's an integral part of Freinet's *Techniques de Vie*.[1]

2. Internal Regulations

The internal rules of the Freinet schools refer to the ones under which the public schools operate. The rules include specifics regarding the cooperative workings of the Freinet schools, consistent with the present and future authorized texts, and to respect the International Convention of Children's Rights. These rules also recognize the fundamental liberties of children while guaranteeing their rights to safety, protection and conditions for a free and responsible movement within the school.

Teachers participate in the children's committees to allow for a cooperative and democratic approach to the management of work and life of the school by those who live and work there. They work out their own rules of conduct in each school's classroom. This cooperative life allows children to manage class/ school projects.

3. The Cooperative Management of the Freinet Teams

These are the basic principles on how to make this organization work:

• The teams must be coherent and adhere to the cooperative spirit that is advocated by Freinet's pedagogy. Those managing the cooperative effort must offer an effective alternative to the traditional mandate
• In order to see this effort work, each pedagogic team must perform its assigned task in a very responsive manner. All team members must be able to use their skills responsibly and for the good of the team
• As far as the management of the school and team organization are concerned (decisions to make, projects to discuss, solving problems, information to share), the teams must meet on a regular basis, above and beyond their mandatory organizational meetings
• Distribution and sharing of tasks: It is imperative that the individuals —to whom various tasks are assigned—assume full responsibilities.

At the start of each school year, the different management tasks (administrative and educational) are listed, and circulated among the members of the team. This organizational chart is then distributed to the local partners. The Freinet teams functioning in the existing lycées and collèges work in close cooperation with the administrative teams.

4. How Are the Teams Formed in the Freinet Schools?
In the schools, the teams formed must abide by the following rules:

• Teachers-members of the Cooperative Council make the decisions
• Elected/chosen members of each team implement those decisions
• The council of teachers guarantees the efficiency of the school.

To become a part of the Freinet teams, the candidates must follow these rules:

• All vacancies in the Freinet teams must be listed with personnel
• People interested in these vacancies must contact the team(s) prior to announcing their candidacy in order to avoid potential conflicts
• A meeting is organized among candidates and teams
• Serious candidates must adhere to the Charter guiding the Freinet and the Modern School, and sign a binding contract of cooperation with that school
• As soon as the list of interested candidates is announced, the cooperative will select those skills that closely match the schools' requirements.

5. Assessing the Freinet Teams
Working in a Freinet team implies a transformation of views on teaching. They are part of a Freinet team which is an evolutionary movement, and a system where all team members are jointly held responsible for its "good working." The team defines its objectives following a report that analyzes the needs of the schools and their students and how to best utilize the pedagogical tools advocated by Freinet and his ICEM *(Institut Coopératif de l'École Moderne),* that will provide all the necessary pedagogical tools. The assessment of these teams is necessary and must take into account the following:

• The projects the team is thinking of implementing
• Making sure that all projects are done in an orderly manner
• The innovations introduced make their success even more important
• The formative aspect of teamwork.

The assessment of a cooperative team's work must take into account all the school projects, how their implementation and completion will open new educational leads and paths to research; it is not based on any individual achievement.

6. The Training and Formation Among the Teams

Before starting, every project must be reviewed with all the participants as a basis for other projects. The Freinet teams perform pedagogical research at various sites, such as selected universities, INRP,[2] CEMEA[3] and CLIMOPE.[4] To reach its goals, the team can call on other partners (specialists, researchers) and must be able to manage many projects with the participation of people from the neighborhood, the school district and the parents. All Freinet teams maintain regular exchanges and participate in national, regional and departmental meetings set up in conjunction with the ICEM/Freinet Pedagogy and the educational plans from the Ministry of the National Education. These teams must always welcome, on a contract basis, individuals and institutions that express an interest in introducing the Freinet Pedagogy in their own milieu.

7. Developing Relationships with Partners, Parents, and Others

The cooperative organization of teams implies recognition of the outstanding features of the different partners and the creation of new relationships. The Freinet teams must learn to create:

A. Relationships with the local community:
• Recognize the importance of cooperative direction
• Recognize that the Charter of the Freinet teams—and the specific character of educational research which ensues—implies that all the local personnel (food handlers, day-care personnel, various teachers and their supervisors) must take into account the school's educational projects and follow its rules, including participating in meetings and talking with the educational teams.
B. Successful relationships with parents:
• Make sure that the school is open to parents in order to construct with them an educational project that will take into account their requests, their waiting, the interests of their children, the look and content of the official texts from the Ministry of National Education, the Charter of the Freinet teams and the International Convention of Children's Rights
• Make sure that these teams give the possibility to parents to collaborate and participate in all school's activities and extra-curricular ones.

C. Successful relationships with trade unions and parents' groups:
• It is important to note that recognizing the charter of the Freinet schools doesn't give an advantage to the schools and its personnel, but it allows them to be inspired by his goals
• The crucial link between the ICEM/Freinet Pedagogy, the trade unions and federations of parents makes it possible to be able to put in place projects that will succeed and to guarantee the respect of this charter by the local communities because the traditional school role is changing.
D. Relationships with the community and the school's neighborhood:
• The school must open its windows to the surrounding world, and that the educational teams must open this world to the children and the teenagers and make their lives part of the school's life
• It is quite important that regular and constructive exchanges between schools, districts, villages and families are necessary in order to create a permanent educational space.

8. Contacts Governing the Cooperation of the Freinet Teams

The educational teams, under the aegis of the ICEM/Freinet Pedagogy, are comprised of teachers functioning under Freinet's pedagogical tenets who respect the orientation and fundamental principles. The teams' members apply themselves to working on the school's specific educational projects.

A. Principles under which the teams work:
• The organization that makes decisions is the team of teachers, in tandem with the Cooperative Council. It is an entity of cooperative reflection, decision and functions. All voices are equal.
• Decisions are taken by a majority of team members and applied to all
• The council meets on a regular basis. It maintains a file that includes all decisions made. If need be, it can meet at a member's special request.
• The absent members can consult files to see what decisions were made
• All teachers participate in the educational life of the school: conferences and open door meetings with outside partners
• The teams put in place the objectives, the techniques and the necessary educational tools for training.
• Councils of teachers and work commissions will be dedicated to the exchanges of educational ideas.
• The distribution of the teachers will vary according to the projects, number of students and the follow-up projects.

B. What are the constraints?
• There are many constraints in working on a Freinet team, and they are defined according to how the projects are set up. Some of these are:
• Availability of time
• Involvement in weekly meetings of the educational team, above and beyond the regularly scheduled meetings
• Numerous dialogues between teachers, social services, and parents, particularly parents who have children with problems
• Opening the minds to research
• Facility to adjust its educational action, based on team results
• Desire to work as practitioner-researcher within the scope of the Freinet pedagogy
• Attending ICEM/Freinet Pedagogy seminars to hone their skills
• Accepting the principle that tasks, traditionally assigned to the director, will be shared by the director of the administrative team.

Where Are the Freinet Schools? How to Find Them?

The constantly updated source for finding schools in France and other parts of the world can be found at *www.freinet.org* the official Web site for the Freinet movement. Roger Auffrand's book *Changer L'École* [5] with its own Web site, is another excellent source for details on the Freinet Pedagogy.

NOTES

1. *Technique de Vie* = life's techniques (publication founded by C. Freinet)
2. Institut National de Recherche Pédagogique (INRP) = National Institute of Pedagogical Research, Paris.
3. Centre d'Entrainement aux Méthodes d'Éducation Active (CEMEA) = Center for active teaching methods.
4. Comité de Liaison des Mouvements Pédagogiques et d'Éducation (CLIMOPE) or Group coordinating all pedagogic and education movements.
5. Auffrand, Roger. *Changer L'École. La pédagogie Freinet.* p. 61-84. Édition Agence Informations Enfance. Saint-Ouen. *http://ecolesdifferentesfree.fr*

Chapter 5
Conclusion

It takes 100 years to discover a good idea,
Another 100 to understand it,
And still another 100 to put it in practice.
—Otto Ludwig (1813-1865)

As this study has shown, Freinet was a genius and pragmatist. Though he was an innovator in the classroom and producer of unique educational material, as the creator of a movement, he could generalize his concepts and ideas successfully. Freinet believed that his widespread pedagogy had the means to transform humanity and surmount capitalism by educating the masses, thus overcoming the nefarious effects of the other classrooms educating "the elite."

To a certain extent, Freinet was more than an educator. He was also a politician and an agitator. He wanted to replace the official schoolbooks with student-produced educational material, thus renovating the teaching methods foisted by a higher order on society.

These changes couldn't take place through only speeches or texts, but they had to provide a combination of critical thinking, writing and technical knowledge: Freinet felt that using a printing press in his classroom was that technique, and was the best blueprint to combine the thought process and the written communication.

The Greatness of Freinet

Extrapolating Freinet's practical philosophy from reading his academic texts was difficult and quite a task since Freinet was a well-read individual, an incisive thinker, a prolific writer, and difficult to pigeon-hole. He described his method of thinking and teaching in *L'Éducation du Travail* (Work as Education), *Les Dits de Mathieu* (Mathieu's Sayings), *L'Essai de Psychologie Sensible* (Essay on Applied Psychology) and *L'École Moderne Française* (French Modern School). Although Freinet's teaching is a blend of concrete, sensitive and stirring ideas, the depth of Freinet's philosophy evolved by inhaling, assimilating, and transforming philosophical and educational currents of his time.

He became involved in reflexology, cybernetics, naturism and structuralism. He added to his already acquired culture by studying at the École Normale de Nice—and preparing to become a school inspector—the ideas of many educators and thinkers of his time: Adolphe Ferrière, Ovide Decroly, Roger Cousinet, Édouard Claparède, Robert Dottrens, Henri Wallon, and Henri Barbusse.

Freinet as a Philosopher

Toward the end of his life, he became involved with a group of educational theoreticians in a short-lived magazine called *Tagore*. This was a radical departure for him because the group believed in the gentler philosophical ideas of Pierre Teilhard de Chardin, a Jesuit philosopher.

Who Was Pierre Teilhard de Chardin (1881-1955)?

He was a French Jesuit priest, paleontologist, and philosopher. He lectured in science at the Jesuit College in Cairo, became a professor of geology at the Catholic Institute (*Institut Catholique*) in Paris, and studied at the Institute of Human Paleontology at the Museum of Natural History[1] in Paris. In 1922, he obtained his doctorate, and left France in 1923 on a paleontology expedition to China, where he stayed until 1946.

His major work, *The Phenomenon of Man*[2] was published posthumously and is based on his scientific thinking, in which he argues that humanity is in a continuous process of evolution toward a perfect spiritual state. Today, he is best known for his unique evolutionary cosmology theories, which supporters believe predicted the arrival of a global Internet more than a half-century before its creation. According to de Chardin, humankind achievements—the only realized purposes in the universe—could only be secured, and advanced through a global network of collective minds.

Freinet's philosophy evolved from de Chardin's "cosmic vision" from his 1955 book *Le Phénomène Humain*. Freinet talks about it in his 1956 book, *Les Méthodes Naturelles Dans la Pédagogie Moderne*[3]. The essence of Freinet's philosophy is detailed in *Les Techniques de Vie*. He expresses his fundamental distrust of everything that is formal, scholastic, rigid, forced and artificial, and he placed his confidence only in nature and mankind.

Although Freinet was influenced by Jean-Jacques Rousseau and his "return to nature," it was really his own peasant's upbringing, his permanent contact with nature, his belief in a "job well done," the feeding of his soul in the warmth of a small community that brings out pride, honesty, and devotion to his career and avocation, which influenced him the most. In his philosophy, Freinet expresses his love of children and his worries about their growth and happiness.

To fully understand the emotional roots of such a philosophy, it is almost imperative to have lived in the rustic, sunny setting of the Freinet school in Vence, among half-naked, laughing, and vibrant children running in the woods of the High-Alps of Provence or paddling in the clear water of the pond. It is this environment that molded Freinet's character and his deep sense of authenticity and conviviality that he maintained throughout his lifetime. This is the reason why the Freinet School has nothing in common with a typical urban school where students are shut in between four walls with only asphalted courtyards and not big enough to allow them freedom or mobility.

In his 1950 book, *Essai de Psychologie Sensible Appliquée à l'Éducation*, Freinet details his psycho-pedagogical ideas (experimental "trial and error") that are behind his method/technique. To Freinet, the schools and teachers are here to teach, but it can only take place if the students want to learn. "You can lead a horse to water, but you cannot make him drink," so the saying goes.

Freinet and the Internet

Because Freinet pioneered printing in the classroom, the school newspaper and the interscholastic correspondence, it is reasonable to think that he would have allowed and encouraged his students to use scanners, e-mail and all the possibilities the Internet has to offer as teaching and learning tools. He introduced printing, the newspaper and the Interscholastic Exchanges to give students the opportunity to increase their knowledge of the written language, as well as developing their thirst for knowledge and information to help them become better citizens. Freinet was the real father of today's online teaching.

The real crux of the Freinet Method was to motivate reading and writing while putting the students in charge of their own learning. Although predicted by de Chardin in 1955, Freinet would have embraced the Internet, as we know it today. The arrival of the Internet and related technologies in all classrooms would have given an added dimension to Freinet's teaching.

Most importantly, electronic mail allows students to quickly exchange messages with correspondents from all over the world and to attach, if needed, drawings, photos, sound and video files. They would have replaced the cultural packets exchanged by mail. Unfortunately, sampling *crêpes* from Brittany or delicious *nougats de Montélimar* must still be exchanged by regular mail!

Moreover, if the classroom's structure had allowed it, receiving and treating the information (sorting, communicating the mail to the recipients, deciding when to answer, developing answers, obtaining the necessary information) is similar to what the students did in the Freinet classes pre-Internet . . . but now they do it faster and with more correspondents. Freinet would probably be rapt with joy to see his busy-bee students write, print and publish in the classrooms, amidst the organized mayhem that he loved so much.

Freinet and His Legacy: 1954-1966

For the first fifty-eight years of his life, Freinet had accomplished much, but he was not finished. He was far from lying down after the battles he had with:

- The French establishment (various Ministers of National Education)
- The Extreme-Right (mayor of Saint-Paul and his supporters)
- Surviving two wars (1914-18 and 1939-45) that resulted in him being grievously wounded (WWI) and interned in a camp (WWII)
- The French Communist Party.

Freinet successfully established his Interscholastic Exchanges with a great number of schools across France and other European countries. These are some of his accomplishments while in his "twilight years" until his untimely death on October 8, 1966:

- With his wife, Élise, he re-started an art program geared toward kindergarten students (*La pratique de l'art enfantin dans les classes*)
- For those teachers, he created a publication in 1951 called *Art Enfantin*
- He re-started a very energetic campaign in 1955 demanding a maximum of twenty-five children per classroom
- He created the FIMEM in 1957
- He arduously campaigned for the French Post Office to give franking privileges for his Interscholastic Exchanges. This campaign started in the early 1960s

• He created in 1964 "programming boxes" (*boîtes enseignantes*) to simulate teaching via a computer – prior to the advent of computers in classrooms
• With Professor Louis Legrand, he founded the journal *Techniques of Life* who had the goal of explain the philosophical cornerstone of Freinet pedagogy to the skeptics in his world of education
• He organized and inspired thirteen Freinet movement national conventions, but was unable to attend the one in 1966 in Perpignan because of his illness
• He organized, every summer in Vence, seminars for Freinet teachers, famous educators, and many pedagogues who came from all over the world to learn from the master himself.

Freinet Is Still Relevant Today

Although Freinet died in 1966, it does not mean that we have to revere and agree with everything he said and wrote, but he still "speaks" to us through his legacy and those who carry on his torch. A dialogue with him can be fruitful as we face the contemporary challenges of providing our own ideas.

These ideas should include the elements he addressed: the role of education, a concrete grasp of life in classrooms and the world, an understanding of human intelligence and psychology, articulation of social ideals, role of technology, and most importantly the proper role and commitment of teachers in the classrooms. Additionally, Freinet is worth listening to because the twenty-first century has started on several jarring notes that refocus our attention on themes he made prominent: interconnection, interdependence and interaction. The classroom is not a scene of isolated agents, it is a world where we are all interconnected, interactive and interdependent.

The last decades of the twentieth century have also witnessed a surge in democratic aspirations. Whether it is the fall of communism in Europe or the success of popularly elected governments in Latin America and other parts of the world, indications point to a deep desire among people to live in democratic societies and break free from dictators' yokes.

A crucial aspect of Freinet's pedagogical tenets was to educate children of oppressed masses, and these ideas take on a new urgency. Freinet could serve as one of the foremost twenty-first century sources of inspiration. Such considerations indicate that the terrain he prepared is that within which we continue to toil.

Conclusion

The continuous study of his endeavor has been a sympathetic one because this author believes that Freinet has laid a landscape from which we can reap a rich intellectual harvest. It is a landscape that would also recognize the changes in time and context. We are no longer in a 1924 rural French village in the High-Alps, but a highly complex technological society in the twenty-first century. Freinet was a complex thinker who held together many strands that we might no longer think blend particularly well. As we are now in this new century, we must choose which strands to emphasize and which to leave behind.

This has been an effort to understand Freinet via the filter provided by his environment and his writing, by those educators who influenced him and by this author's deep sense of wanting to provide a forum for discussion because, if it is not for Freinet, using computers, fax machines and e-mail as educational tools, might have never happened. This author acknowledges his gratitude to Freinet as he changed his life!

NOTES

1. Institut de Paléontologie Humaine au Musée d'Histoire Naturelle (Paris).
2. *Le Phénomène Humain*, written 1938-1940.
3. Natural Methods in Modern Pedagogy.

Chapter 6
Selected Bibliography

I. Printing Press

Freinet, Célestin. "Vers l'École du prolétariat. Contre un enseignement livresque: l'imprimerie à l'École." *Clarté*. 75. 259-61. Juin 1925.

———. "Vie pédagogique: L'imprimerie à l'école." *L'École Émancipée*. 41. 8 juillet 1925.

———. "Vie pédagogique: Mes impressions de pédagogue en Russie soviétique (suite)" & "Vie scolaire: L'imprimerie à l'école." *L'École Émancipée*. 7. 8 novembre 1925.

———. "Vie scolaire: Une expérience d'adaptation de notre enseignement:L'imprimerie à l'école (suite)." *L'École Émancipée*. 8. 15 novembre 1925.

———. "Vie scolaire: L'imprimerie à l'école." *L'École Émancipée*. 93-95. 4 juillet 1926.

Villermoz, Eugène. "A l'École de Gutenberg." *Le Temps*. 1. 4 juillet 1926.

Freinet, Célestin. "Deuxième lettre circulaire aux classes travaillant avec l'imprimerie." *L'imprimerie à l'École*. 24 octobre 1926.

———. L'Imprimerie à l'École. E. Ferrary, Éditeur. Boulogne (Seine). Décembre 1926.

———. "La Vie Pédagogique: L'imprimerie à l'école." *Notre Arme*. 48. 6-7. Décembre 1926.

———. "Notre situation." *L'Imprimerie à l'École*. Bulletin 2. Décembre 1926.

Aicard, J. "Bibliographie: Un livre à lire: 'L'imprimerie à l'école' (C. Freinet)." *Notre Arme*. 52. Février 1927.

Freinet, Célestin. "Les échanges." *L'Imprimerie à l'École*. Bulletin 3. Février 1927.

Ferrière, Ad. "L'imprimerie à l'école primaire." *Pour L'Ère Nouvelle*. 26. 60-61. Mars 1927.

Freinet, Célestin. "La Gerbe." *L'Imprimerie à l'École*. Bulletin 4. Avril 1927.

———. "Organisation." *L'Imprimerie à l'École*. Bulletin 5. Mai 1927.

Freinet, Célestin. "L'imprimerie à l'école" & "les échanges internationaux." *L'Internationale de l'Enseignement,* N° 9. 29-31. Juin 1927.

――――. "Matériel d'Imprimerie." *L'Imprimerie à l'École.* Bulletin 6. 1-4. Juin 1927.

――――. "Vie Pédagogique: La correspondance interscolaire réalisée par l'imprimerie à l'École" & "Cinémathèque coopérative." *L'École Émancipée.* 38. 19 juin 1927.

――――. "Cempuis: Un essai d'éducation prolétarienne au XIXᵉ Siècle." *L'Internationale de l'Enseignement.* 1. 28-29. Octobre 1927.

――――. "La Vie Corporative: Les conférences pédagogiques & L'imprimerie à l'école." *Notre Arme.* 55. 2-3. 8. Octobre 1927.

――――. "Circulaire aux adhérents." *L'Imprimerie à l'École.* 3. 2 pages. Octobre 1927.

――――. "Congrès de Tours et compte-rendu des travaux de l'année 1926-1927". *L'Imprimerie à l'École.* Bulletin 7. Octobre 1927.

――――. "Congrès de Tours et compte-rendu des travaux de l'année 1926-1927 (suite)." *L'Imprimerie à l'École.* Bulletin 8. Novembre 1927.

――――. "Circulaire aux adhérents." *L'Imprimerie à l'École.* 4. 2 pages. Novembre 1927.

――――. "La Cinémathèque coopérative de films Pathé-Baby et L'imprimerie à l'école." *Fédération Unitaire de L'Enseignement.* 56-8. 1928.

――――. "Circulaire aux adhérents." *L'Imprimerie à l'École.* 6. 2 pages. Janvier 1928.

Lagier-Bruno, M-L. "Vie Pédagogique: La rédaction libre à l'école primaire." *L'École Émancipée.* 29. 470-71. 15 avril 1928.

――――. "Vie Pédagogique: La rédaction libre à l'école primaire II." *L'École Émancipée.* 30. 487-88. 22 avril 1928.

Freinet, Célestin. "Vers une méthode nouvelle pour les écoles populaires." *L'Imprimerie à l'École.* Bulletin 18. Décembre 1928.

――――. Conte de la Veillée. Les enfants de l'École de Bar-sur-Loup. 22 décembre 1928. *[Copie envoyée à l'inspecteur d'académie Brunet.]*

――――. "Vie Pédagogique: 'Plus de manuels scolaires!'"*L'École Émancipée.* 13. 212-13. 23 décembre 1928.

――――. "Vie Pédagogique: Réalisateurs révolutionnaires." *L'École Émancipée.* 18. 290-91. 27 janvier 1929.

――――. "L'imprimerie à l'école." *Monde.* 51. 11. 25 mai 1929.

――――. "L'imprimerie à l'école." *Pour L'Ère Nouvelle.* 49. 165-67. Juillet-août 1929.

Freinet, Célestin. "La rationalisation dans l'enseignement." *Monde*. 73. 13. 26. octobre 1929.

————. "Programme de travail." *L'Imprimerie à l'École*. Bulletin 35. Octobre 1930.

————. "Correspondances scolaires internationales." Circulaire. *L'Imprimerie à l'École*. Novembre 1930.

————. "Théories pédagogiques et techniques pédagogiques."*L'Imprimerie à l'École*. Bulletin 38. Janvier 1931.

————. "La coopération scolaire." *L'Imprimerie à l'École*. Bulletin 50. Mars 1932.

————. "Psychanalyse et éducation." *L'Imprimerie à l'École*. Bulletin 51. Avril 1932.

————. "Vers l'avenir!" *L'Imprimerie à l'École*. Bulletin. 52. Mai 1932.

————."Une technique nouvelle de travail scolaire par l'imprimerie à l'école." *Pour L'Ère Nouvelle*. 99. 174-78. Juillet 1934.

————. "L'imprimerie à L'école: L'École Freinet." *L'Éducateur Prolétarien*. 17. 381-86. Mai 1935.

————. "L'imprimerie à l'école. L'organisation et l'évolution de l'École Freinet." *L'Éducateur Prolétarien*. 5. 97-100. 10 décembre 1935.

Wallon, Henri. "Allocution au Congrès de Cheltenham (Grande-Bretagne) pour introduire 'L'imprimerie à l'école' et C. Freinet." *Pour L'Ère Nouvelle*. 121. 245-46. Octobre 1936.

Freinet, Célestin. Discours au Congrès de Cheltenham sur 'L'imprimerie à l'école'. *Pour L'Ère Nouvelle*. 121. 246-53. Octobre 1936.

————. "L'École en Norvège. L'imprimerie à l'école: diffusion mondiale de notre technique." *L'Éducateur Prolétarien*. 3-4. Novembre 1936.

————. "La Technique Freinet." *BENP*. 1. Septembre 1937.

Barré, G. "Chez l'inventeur de l'imprimerie à l'école: une visite à M. Freinet." *L'École Bernoise/Berner Schulblatt*. 34. 592-94. 19 novembre 1938.

Freinet, Célestin."Nos échanges interscolaires." *L'Éducateur Prolétarien*. Décembre 1938.

————. "L'imprimerie à l'école." *L'Éducateur*. 5. 65-66. (Censuré). 1er décembre 1939.

Freinet, Célestin. et L. Balesse. "La lecture par l'imprimerie à l'école." *BEM*. 7. Cannes. 1961.

Guérin, Pierre, Debarbieux, E. et al. Pédagogie Freinet: de l'imprimerie à l'imprimante. 192. *L'Éducateur*. Supplément. 8. Mai 1987.

II. Interscholastic Exchanges

Buisson, Ferdinand, éd. Dictionnaire de Pédagogie et d'Instruction Primaire. Hachette. Paris. 1882.

Freinet, Célestin. "Echanges de cartes postales." *Notre Arme.* 12. 12. Janvier 1923.

———. "Cahiers roulants." *Notre Arme.* 13. 12. Février–mars 1923.

———. "L'Action pédagogique: Cahiers roulants; Collection de vues; Renseignements."*Notre Arme.* 15. 11–12. Juin 1923.

———. "Cahiers roulants."*Notre Arme.* 21. 12. Février 1924.

Ringel, Martin. "Appel pour la formation d'échange d'un pays à l'autre." *L'Internationale de l'Enseignement.* 2. 55. Novembre 1926.

Freinet, Célestin. "Les échanges." *L'Imprimerie à l'École.* Bulletin 3. Février 1927.

———. "Vie Pédagogique: La correspondance interscolaire réalisée par l'imprimerie à l'École" et "Cinémathèque coopérative."*L'École Émancipée.* 38. 19 juin 1927.

———. "L'imprimerie à l'école" et "les échanges internationaux." *L'Internationale de l'Enseignement.* 9. 29–31. Juin 1927.

———. "L'organisation des échanges." *L'Imprimerie à l'École.* Bulletin 9. Décembre 1927.

———. "Correspondances scolaires internationales." Circulaire. *L'Imprimerie à l'École.* Novembre 1930.

———. "Théories pédagogiques et techniques pédagogiques." *L'Imprimerie à l'École.* Bulletin. 38. Janvier 1931.

———. Lettres à M. Marius Monzeglio "lui demandant que son fils,Louis, restitue une carte d'un correspondant russe qui appartient à la classe." Saint-Paul. 26 et 29 avril 1932.

De Monzie, Anatole. Lettre à la Direction de l'Enseignement Primaire demandant "de me faire connaître l'attitude à prendre à l'égard d'une correspondance interscolaire avec les soviets." Paris. 16 juillet 1932.

Freinet, Célestin."Une technique nouvelle de travail scolaire par l'imprimerie à l'école." *Pour L'Ère Nouvelle.* 99. 174–78. Juillet 1934.

———. "La Technique Freinet." *BENP.* 1. Septembre 1937.

———. "Nos échanges interscolaires." *L'Éducateur Prolétarien.* Décembre 1938.

Freinet, Célestin et S. Carmilet. "Correspondance interscolaire." *L'Éducateur.* 4. 58–59. 15 novembre 1945.

Séclet-Riou, Fernande. Lettre à Maurice Pigeon louant les techniques Freinet. Paris. 3 janvier 1946.

Freinet, Célestin et H. Alziary. "Les correspondances interscolaires." *BENP*. 32. Novembre 1947.

Freinet, Célestin. "Nos échanges interscolaires." *L'Éducateur*. 16. 15 mai 1948.

———. "Correspondance interscolaire." *L'Éducateur*. 1. 1er octobre. 1948.

———. "Correspondance interscolaire." *L'Éducateur*. 2. 15 octobre. 1948.

———. "Correspondance interscolaire." *L'Éducateur*. 3. Novembre 1948.

———. "Correspondance interscolaire." *L'Éducateur*. 1. 1er octobre 1949.

———. "Une pédagogie moderne basée sur une puissante motivation: Les échanges interscolaires." *L'Éducateur*. 19. 15 juin 1950.

———. "Une aventure unique dans la pédagogie." *L'Éducateur*. 20. 1er juillet 1950.

———. "Correspondances interscolaires." *L'Éducateur*. 1. 1er octobre 1950.

Denjean, R. et P. Guérin. "Voyage-échange international." *BENP*. 60. Mars 1951

Freinet, Célestin. "Les échanges interscolaires. *L'Éducateur*. 1er octobre 1951.

Freinet, Célestin, R. Denjean et al. "Pour l'officialisation des voyages-échanges interscolaires." *BENP*. 76. Novembre 1952.

Freinet, Célestin. "Les Techniques Freinet." *BENP*. 80. Mars 1953.

———. "La correspondance interscolaire." *L'Éducateur*. 1. 1er octobre 1953.

———. "Correspondance internationale." *L'Éducateur*. 3. 1er novembre 1953.

———. "Cahiers de roulement interscolaire." *L'Éducateur*. Supplément au 2. 15 octobre 1958.

———. "Les Techniques Freinet." *L'Éducateur*. Supplément au 3. 2–8. 1er novembre 1958.

Fonvieille, Raymond. La Correspondance Interscolaire. ICEM-FIMEM. *L'Éducateur*. 25, 14. Octobre 1959.

———. La Correspondance Interscolaire. ICEM-FIMEM. *L'Éducateur*. 26, 14. Novembre 1959.

Freinet, Célestin. "Le service des correspondances interscolaires internationales." *L'Éducateur*. 1. 1er octobre 1962

———. "Le service des correspondances interscolaires nationales." *L'Éducateur*. 16–17. 1er –15 octobre 1964.

Berteloot, Clémence, D. Gervilliers et al. "Les correspondances scolaires." *BEM*. 50–53. 1968.

Lavergne, M. "Une correspondance scolaire vraiment internationale." *L'Éducateur*. 6. 1er mars 1968.

Freinet Élise et Michel Launay. *Centre de Recherches et d'Échanges Universitaires* (CREU). Freinet et la coopération. 2. 19-33. Janvier-mars 1977.

Portier, Henri. "René Daniel, premier correspondant de Freinet." *Amis de Freinet*. 60. 12–14. Décembre 1993.

III. Books Written by Célestin and Élise Freinet

Freinet, Célestin. L'École Moderne Française. Editions Ophrys. Gap. 1945.

———. Le Journal Scolaire. Editions Rossignol. Montmorillon. 1957.

———. Essai de Psychologie Sensible. Delachaux & Niestlé.Neuchâtel.1966.

———. Les Techniques Freinet de l'École Moderne. Librairie Armand-Colin. Paris. 1969.

———. Souvenirs d'enfance (inédit). *Amis de Freinet*. 11. 26-38. 15 février-1ᵉʳ mars 1972.

Freinet, Élise. L'École Freinet: Réserve d'enfants. PCM/petite collection maspero. Paris. 1974.

———. L'itinéraire de Célestin Freinet. petite bibliothèque payot. Paris. 1977.

Freinet, Célestin. Pour l'École du peuple. François Maspero. Paris. 1977.

———. L'Éducation du travail. Delachaux & Niestlé. Neuchâtel. 1978.

———. La santé mentale de l'enfant. François Maspero. Paris. 1979.

Freinet, Élise. Vers Un Monde Fraternel. Freinet, Ferrière et l'École Moderne. 10. 5. Octobre 1979.

Freinet, Célestin. Oeuvres Pédagogiques. Édition établie par Madeleine Freinet. Introduction de Jacques Bens. Tomes I & II. Éd. du Seuil. Paris. 1994.

> Tome I: L'Education du Travail (1942-1943)
> Essai de Psychologie Sensible (1950)
> Tome II: L'École Moderne Française (1943)
> Les Dits de Mathieu (1946-1954)
> Méthode Naturelle de Lecture (1961)
> Les Invariants Pédagogiques (1964)
> Méthode Naturelle de Dessin (1951)
> Les Genèses (1953-1964)

IV. Books and Other Media Inspired by Célestin Freinet

Husson, J. Théoriciens et pionniers de l'Education nouvelle. *L'Éducateur*. 19.(numéro spécial). 1ᵉʳ juillet 1946.

———. L'Education Decroly.*L'Éducateur*. (numéro spécial). 26. Février 1947.

Husson, J. *BENP*. Bakulé. 33. Décembre 1947.

———. *BENP*. Paul Robin, Éducateur. 44. Mars 1949.

Le Chanois, Jean-Paul. L'École Buissonnière. Réalisateur et directeur d'un film décrivant un instituteur de campagne (Freinet) dans les années 1920-1922. 110 minutes. 1949.

Gouzil, Marcel. La Vie et l'Oeuvre de Célestin Freinet. *Bulletin Mensuel du Syndicat des Instituteurs Publiques*. 3. 38-40. Décembre 1956.

Boyau, R. Vie Scolaire: Célestin Freinet. *L'École Émancipée*. 4. 25-26. 5 octobre 1966.

Alziary, Honoré, Michel Barré, et al. Sur la mort de Freinet. *Techniques de Vie*. 73. 1ᵉʳ novembre 1966.

Vial, Jean.Freinet, mon maître. *L'École et La Vie*. 4. 1-5. 5 novembre 1966.

Guignet, J.P., R.Dottrens et al. Célestin Freinet. *Éducateur et Bulletin Corporatif (Lausanne)*. 39. 11 novembre 1966.

Avanzini, G., É. Freinet, M. Suchère, C. et M. Berteloot. Hommage à Freinet. *Société Binet & Simon*. 494. 1967.

Prudencio, Eustache. Pédagogie Vivante. Vers l'École Moderne Africaine: Techniques Freinet. Editions Silva, Cotonou (Benin). 1967.

Piaton, Georges. La Pensée Pédagogique de Célestin Freinet. Édition Privat. Toulouse. 1974.

Snyders, Georges. Pédagogie progressiste. PUF. Paris. 1975.

Avanzini, Guy (éd.). L'avenir du Mouvement Freinet. *Société Binet & Simon*. 557. Octobre-décembre 1977.

Institut Coopératif de l'École Moderne. Perspectives d'Education populaire. PCM/petite collection maspero. Paris. 1979.

Faure, Raoul. L'École Moderne Française: Techniques et pédagogie Freinet. Le Cric (Grenoble). 1985.

Gonnet, Jacques. Les journaux produits par les jeunes en age scolaire. Thèse de Doctorat. Université de Bordeaux III. 1985.

Semenowicz, Halina. Célestin et Élise Freinet: Bibliographie Internationale (1920-1978). INRP. Paris. 1986.

Barré, Michel, P. Badin et al. BT2. Célestin Freinet et l'École Moderne. 193. Janvier 1987.

Thomas, Emile, Le Gal J., Le Bohec, P. et al. L'Éducateur. Célestin Freinet: 20 ans plus tard. 190-91. Supplément au 6 de mars 1987.

Clanché, Pierre, et Testanière, J. (eds.) Actualité de la Pédagogie Freinet. Presses Universitaires de Bordeaux. 1987.

INRP-Musée National de l'Education. Célestin Freinet et sa pédagogie. Exposition à Rouen 1987-1988.

Korczak, Janus. La Gazette Scolaire. Traduit du polonais par Z. Bobowicz. Edité par le CLEMI. Paris. 1988.

Barré, Michel. Chronologie de l'École Moderne: Quelle est la date d'origine du mouvement? *Amis de Freinet.* 52. 18-22. Décembre 1989.

———. Rendre à Élise Freinet la part qui lui revient. *Amis de Freinet.* 54. Décembre 1990.

Piaton, Georges. De Decroly à Freinet: Un modèle d'école. *Société Binet-Simon.* 623. 116-25. 1990.

Debarbieux, Éric., J. Gilbert et al. La philosophie de Freinet. *Le Nouvel Éducateur.* 222. Janvier 1991.

Barré, Michel. La jeunesse de Célestin Freinet. *Amis de Freinet.* 55. 29-38. Juin 1991.

Guihaumé, Claude. Les origines de 'l'imprimerie à l'école': 1926-1930. *Bulletin de la Société d'Agriculture.* Le Mans (Sarthe). 1991.

Landroit H. et F. Dubreucq. Le Docteur Decroly et Célestin Freinet. Colloque de l'Education Populaire. Université de Liège (Belgique). Novembre 1991.

Association "Les Amis de Jean Lévi." Les Écoles différentes. Saint-Brice-Sous-Forêt. 1992.

Maury, Liliane. Freinet et la pédagogie. PUF. Paris. 1993.

Bizieau, Charles et A. Lefeuvre. La Pédagogie Freinet est Internationale. Le *Nouvel Éducateur.* 50. Juin 1993.

"Sur Célestin Freinet." Profils perdus. Avec Madeleine Bens-Freinet, Jacques Bens, Roger Billé, et des enfants de l'École Freinet de Vence. *France-Culture Radio.* Octobre 1993.

Portier, Henri. René Daniel, premier correspondant de Freinet. *Amis de Freinet.* 60. 12-14. Décembre 1993.

Guihaumé, Claude. Makarenko n'a exercé aucune influence sur Freinet. *Amis de Freinet.* 61. 30-40. Juin 1994.

Peyronie, Henri. Célestin Freinet (1896-1966). 212-26. Dans 'Quinze Pédagogues: Leur influence aujourd'hui.' Edité par Jean Houssaye. Éditions Armand Colin. Paris, 1994.

Legrand, Louis. "Célestin Freinet (1896-1966)." 407-23. Dans 'Perspectives de l'Education.' Édité par Zaghloul Morsy. 85-86. UNESCO. Paris. 1994.

Barré, Michel. Célestin Freinet, un éducateur pour notre temps. PEMF. Tome I: Les années fondatrices. 1995.

Tome II: Vers une alternative pédagogique. 1996.

Boumard, Patrick. Célestin Freinet. Presses Universitaires de France. Paris. 1996.

Acker Victor. *Célestin Freinet (1896-1966): L'Histoire d'un Jeune Intellectuel.* Thèse de doctorat. Université de Haute Bretagne. Rennes. Octobre 1997.

———. Célestin Freinet (A Biography). Greenwood Press. July 2000.

Auffrand, Roger. La Pédagogie Freinet dans 'Des Écoles Différentes: Changer L'École.' 61-85. Édition Agence Informations Enfants. St-Ouen. 2002.

Acker, Victor. Célestin Freinet (1896-1966): L'Histoire d'un Jeune Intellectuel. L'Harmattan. Paris. 2006. ISBN:2-296-00524-1.

Appendix A: Biographical Data

1896   Célestin Freinet is born on October 15 in the small village of Gars (Maritime-Alps) a small village close to Nice and the Italian border.

1912   Freinet takes the entrance exams and is accepted at the *école normale d'instituteurs* of Nice to become an elementary school teacher.

1914   He does not finish his teacher-training education when World War I is declared. Before being drafted, he substitutes for three months at the St-Cézaire (M-A) elementary school.

1915   In April, the army drafts him as an officer-candidate.

1917   In April, he is critically wounded in the battle of *Chemin des Dames* near Soissons (Aisne).[1] In 1920, he writes about his wounds, being near-death and convalescing. [2]

1918   He substitutes in La Croix-Villard, another village in the Maritime-Alps, where he meets Élise Lagier-Bruno, a schoolteacher and a gifted wood engraver, who teaches nearby. He marries her in 1926.

1919   He is appointed adjunct-teacher at the Boys' School of Bar-sur-Loup (M-A), a small town near Grasse (M-A). He joins an anarcho-syndicalist teachers' union and becomes active in their splinter group affiliated with the PCF.

1922   In the summer, Freinet visits the Altona School, near Hamburg, Germany, known as *an anarchist* or *libertarian school*. He does not care for their teaching methods.[3]

1923   In June, he attends the second *Congrès de la Ligue Internationale pour l'Éducation Nouvelle* in Montreux (Switzerland), where he becomes acquainted with Swiss educators from the Institut Jean-Jacques Rousseau of Geneva: Édouard Claparède, Pierre Bovet and Adolphe Ferrière.

1924   In June, he buys a small printing press and, with his students, prints a "free text"[4] of the narrative of the snail race they staged.

1925   In June, with a group of teachers, he visits Russia and meets with its new rulers to lecture on his pedagogical model and travels at length in this country. This trip influenced his future views on education and he wrote extensively on the Soviet pedagogical system.

1926   René Daniel, a teacher in Trégunc-St-Philibert (Brittany), also buys a Cinup printing press in June and becomes Freinet's first regular correspondent. The Interscholastic Exchange is created in October.

1927   In July, he establishes *La Coopérative de L'Enseignement Laïc* (CEL) with the six core members of his movement.

1928   Freinet is appointed director of the elementary school in Saint-Paul-de-Vence (M-A) and publishes many articles on various topics, including Interscholastic Exchanges.

1929   Birth of his daughter, Madeleine. His wife, Élise, is named adjunct-teacher at the Girls' School of Saint-Paul-de-Vence.

1930   The Freinet Movement has now grown to 250 members.

1932- Freinet faces many obstacles created by agitators, politicians and
1934   officials who are opposed to his innovative teaching methods and his Communist leanings.[5] He experiences the rise of fascism. This difficult episode in Freinet's life is usually referenced as 'L'Affaire Saint Paul.'

1935   He is forced to leave public education in Saint-Paul and builds a new school in Vence (M-A) called L'École Freinet.[6] Creates with the French writer Romain Rolland "Le Front de l'Enfance."[7]

1938- L'École Freinet closes during World War II. The Vichy government
1946   of Maréchal Pétain confines Freinet as a known political agitator to the Chibron Work Camp (Var) in March 1940. He is released on October 1941 for poor health[8] and placed under house arrest. He joins the Résistance Movement in 1944. The Freinet School is pillaged and ransacked during the war but reopens late in 1946.

1949   The movie *L'École Buissonnière* [9] is directed by Jean-Paul Le Chanois with a script written by Élise Freinet.[10] This movie, partially financed by the French Communist Party, describes the pedagogical quest of an innovator teacher "Mr. Pascal" (Freinet).

1952- Freinet faces virulent attacks directed by Georges Cogniot and
1954   Georges Snyders of the PCF as being 'too bourgeois'. It causes a wide chasm between him and the PCF.

1966   Freinet passes away in October in Vence and is buried in Gars. The educator Jean Vial said upon hearing the death of his friend:[11] *Freinet est mort. Il est des morts qui vivent . . .Intensément.*[12]

NOTES

1. Famous battle where seventy-five French soldiers were executed for refusing to obey General Robert Nivelle's orders to fight a much superior German army. One of his army comrades was Jacques Doriot who bolted from the PCF (1936) to create the PPF (*Parti Populaire Français*).

2. Célestin Freinet. *Touché. Souvenirs d'un blessé de guerre*. Maison Française d'Art et d' Édition.1920. (Reprinted in 1996)

3. Elisabeth Hughenin. *Paul Geheeb et la Libre Communauté de l'Odenwald*. Édition du Bureau International des Écoles Nouvelles. Genève. 1923.

4. "Free text," or *texte libre* refers to a compilation of the various texts written by the students; it is in apposition to "text books" or "manuel scolaires."

5. Célestin Freinet. "Le scandale scolaire de Saint-Paul." *Notre Arme*. 106. pp. 2-17. Décembre 1932.

6. Célestin Freinet. "Une année à l'École Freinet." *L'Éducateur Prolétarien*. 19–20. pp. 1–32. 10 juillet 1936.

7. Front de l'Enfance = Children's Movement.

8. Adolphe Ferrière. Lettre demandant la libération de Freinet. Avril 1940.

9. Available on DVD in French with English subtitles as "Passion for Life." (Facets Video. Chicago IL).

10. Élise Freinet. "Scénario pour le film L'École Buissonnière." *Bibliothèque de Travail*. 100. Cannes. 22 janvier 1950.

11. Jean Vial. "Freinet, mon maître" *L'École et La Vie*. 4. 5 novembre 1966. pp. 1-5.

12. *Though Freinet is dead, he is among the dead who live passionately.*

Index

Note: Books are in italics

About the Author

VICTOR ACKER, born in a French-speaking household, and educated at the Lycée Français in Alexandria (Egypt), left for Europe after the Suez Canal War (1956), and settled in New York City in 1962. After many years working in advertising and two enjoyable years at The Metropolitan Opera House, he made a career change, obtained an M.A. in Education from NYU and a *Doctorat d'État* from the Université de Haute-Bretagne (Rennes, France) where he presented his thesis in French on Célestin FREINET. After his first book on Freinet was published by Greenwood Press in English, the French Government knighted him *Chevalier dans l'Ordre des Palmes Académiques* for introducing Freinet to the Anglophone world. Although he taught French at John Jay College, and Comparative Literature at Baruch College, he currently teaches English and "Philosophy of Education" at Touro College's Graduate School of Education while pursuing other facets of writing (autobiography and mysteries). He lives in Briarwood, New York with his wife, Carole and their dog, Chloe. This is his third book on Freinet.